THE BEST OF
REMINISCE

CONTENTS

REMINISCE

PICTURED ON FRONT COVER
Family in red car on **178**, Amy Danchisko

Boys in sunglasses on **57**, Ruby Helen Smith

Married couple on **77**, Richard Obrosky

Soldiers on **148**, Harry Wagner

Family photo on **105**, Bill Craft

ADDITIONAL PHOTO CREDITS
Reader-Submitted Images
16 *bl* Katie Blau; **26-27** (owl) Anna Donato; **140-147** (MASH photos) Dr. Hugh Hickey

Stock Images
49 The U.S. National Archives and Records Administration; **84** Campbell Soup Co.; **85** *tr* NASA; **92** Division of Cultural and Community Life, National Museum of American History, Smithsonian Institution; **102**, **103** *tr* OPERATION ® & © 2019 Hasbro, Inc. Used with permission; **107**, **124** Daily Reflector Negative Collection/East Carolina Manuscript Collection/J.Y. Joyner Library; **115** The American Geographical Society Library, University of Wisconsin-Milwaukee Libraries **157**, **162** *b* Courtesy of Library of Congress, LC-DIG-det-4a17430, LC-DIG-det-4a17904; **200** (cover) Thomas More Publishing; **204** *l* National Portrait Gallery, Smithsonian Institution

Getty: **18** H. Armstrong Roberts/ClassicStock; **22** Star Tribune; **34-35** (garden) N8tureGrl; **85** *bl*, **181**, **187**, **188** *t*, **188** *l*, **188** *r*, **197** *rt*, **197** *rb* Bettmann Archive; **100** Jack Mitchell; **111**, **112** *bl*, **113** *bl* Universal Images Group; **118-119** (city) David Shvartsman; **182-183**, **186** *r* Corbis Historical; **192**, **198**, **201** Michael Ochs Archives; **193** Darlene Hammond; **194** Herbert Dorfman; **196** John Springer Collection; **197** *l* Universal History Archive; **200** *t* University of Southern California; **202** Hulton Archive; **203** *t* Underwood Archives; **203** *bl* Sunset Boulevard; **203** *br* Silver Screen Collection, **208** RB

Shutterstock: **93** *br* Thomas Bethge; **103** *bl* Carrie Antlfinger/AP; **184-185**, **186** *l* Everett

Text, photography and illustrations for *The Best of Reminisce 2022* are based on articles previously published in *Reminisce* magazine.

International Standard Book Number:
D 978-1-62145-793-0
U 978-1-62145-794-7

Component Number:
D 117300108H
U 117300110H

Printed in U.S.A.
1 3 5 7 9 10 8 6 4 2

BICYCLE BUILT FOR SIX
After I got home from my job at the post office in the 1960s, I piled Cathy and her brothers Mark, David and Jerry into the bike baskets for a ride around the neighborhood. Even the dog, Spooky, liked it.
GEORGE LABERGE • WESTLAND, MI

Y ears pass and trends change, but the people, places and things that made us who we are remain pristine and preserved in our memories. We hope this keepsake collection of stories and photos from the previous year of *Reminisce* encourages you to reflect on moments in your life that have stood the test of time.

The Best of Reminisce features humorous and heartwarming stories of growing up. You'll also find tales of true love, including sweethearts who wed after knowing each other for just four weeks, and some that reflect on nostalgic fun, such as the excitement of visiting department stores.

We've dedicated a chapter to wartime stories—including the story of one man's father who was part of the unit that inspired *M*A*S*H*.

Of course, we all remember our first jobs. In a chapter dedicated to work, former paper boys and paper girls tell of life on the delivery route.

You'll also find special stories of encounters with famous people, such as a meeting with Babe Ruth in the 1920s, and a woman who met her celebrity crush—Barry Williams—in the '70s.

We're grateful you've chosen to join us as we remember pieces of the past that made us who we are today. Enjoy.

THE EDITORS OF *REMINISCE* MAGAZINE

CHAPTER 1

GROWING UP

Time spent with friends, writing in diaries, bonding with our pet pals and more—it all made us who we are today.

Tree Horse

My dad was chopping down a tree when my siblings and I noticed a rare opportunity. We all climbed onto our new tree horse while Mom grabbed the camera. The photo, from about 1964, shows (from left) me, Melanie, Stephanie and Jon.

DULCIE SHOENER · WHITEFISH BAY, WI

Robert rides shotgun in Dave's MG, with Earl in the back.

Weightlifting Is the Warmup

Friendship stays strong throughout their lifetimes.

My friendship with Earl Hook and Dave Keaggy began when we were in our midteens. I met Earl first, when he introduced himself at a ninth grade football meeting. He was 5 feet 9 inches and had to look up to talk to me. Dave and I met at track practice. Tall and well-built, he had a gym in his garage, and one day I invited Earl to come along to work out. Pumping iron together formed the foundation of a lifelong friendship for the three of us.

In 1965, Earl and I were back in Waterford, Michigan—home from college. Dave knew he would soon be drafted, so instead of waiting for his number to come up, he decided to enlist. He went to the Air Force recruitment center in downtown Pontiac. The office had a sign that said, "Back at 1 p.m." The Army and Navy recruiters were also on their lunch break, but the Marine recruiter was there, so Dave joined the Marine Corps that day.

We spent the summer working, riding Dave's Honda 90 motorcycle to work every day. At night we cruised in his MG with the top down. The night before Dave left for boot camp, we talked most of the night. I got home just before the sun came up.

Dave went to Vietnam in 1966. His dad, Duke, hired me to help with odd jobs— I think having me around helped him cope with Dave's absence. It was painful and traumatic when we learned that one of our high school classmates was killed in Vietnam. Dave was wounded twice during his three tours of duty, and his experience stayed with him. One Fourth of July a firecracker went off near us, and Dave dove for cover.

I got married and graduated in 1969. Earl ended up becoming a science teacher. Dave moved to Arizona, and he worked a variety of jobs. But not even long separations diminished our friendship. When we were together, we picked up right where we had left off.

Earl died in 2019. During weekly visits with him, we had talked for hours about the old days, remembering that long-ago summer when nothing was beyond our reach.

ROBERT DUSTMAN · AUBURN HILLS, MI

Happiness is Being on Stage

Singing along with records was the start of a lifetime of entertaining with music.

From age 3, I was a performer, singing along with records, and for festivals at schools and churches—wherever I could be a hambone. My hero was Elvis, so I learned guitar, as well as piano, saxophone and drums.

I met Debbie Adcox in fifth grade at Farley Elementary School in Paducah. Debbie was also musical, singing and playing piano. I was smitten, but she was reluctant to be my girlfriend. Cooties were a big deal, and I wondered if I had them. Or maybe I was just a blockhead! But I persisted, and by the time we were in high school, we were going steady.

We were Peanuts fans: I had all of the comic books—there weren't many—and a few record albums with the Peanuts gang. I faithfully watched all the TV specials, of course. During our senior year at Reidland High School in 1972, our choral department presented *You're a Good Man, Charlie Brown*. I got the part of Charlie Brown and Debbie was Peppermint Patty.

Even though I was used to being on the stage, acting was a whole new world. It was my first time wearing makeup—I was a little embarrassed, and I wondered what my friends would think. We rehearsed the musical for several weeks. First we rehearsed in the in the choir room, and then on the gym stage where the single performance was held one Friday night.

Debbie and I went on to enjoy a lot more stage time together. We are now married and have traveled extensively, playing music around the country and internationally.

TERRY MIKE JEFFREY · PADUCAH, KY

Terry Mike, holding the bat, and Debbie, far right, were big fans of the Peanuts gang.

SAME AGE INSIDE

John Manney holds on to best pal, Tinker. John, now of Henderson, NV, remembers Tinker as "quite the car chaser."

Inez Torres Evans, 8, has her arms full in San Francisco, CA. Daughter Karen Evans writes that her mother still loves holding babies.

Britt Barkley, now retired from the military and living in San Antonio, TX, was 5 when his dad took this photo of him on a pony in their front yard in Bath, SC.

Cub Scout Jerry Hopkins was 8 and prepared for anything in Hoopeston, IL.

Greer White, now of Naples, FL, was 3 when she gave a smile for the camera in Albany, GA.

Barbara, left, didn't understand all the fuss after she stepped out to buy herself some shoes. Sisters Peggy, Betty and Ruth already had theirs. Their pal Bozo didn't need any.

BARBIE NEEDS A NEW PAIR OF SHOES

GROWING UP IN SAN LUIS OBISPO, California, in the 1950s was a lot of fun. We spent most of our time with our extended family, who all lived near us. My father worked at a corner grocery next to our house. In 1956, my mother had her hands full raising four daughters, with a fifth child on the way. That fall, my older sisters, Ruth and Betty, and I were getting ready to go to Emerson Elementary, which also meant going on a shopping trip for new dresses and shoes.

Three-year-old Barbara, or Barbie, as Aunt Mary called her, must have felt left out. One morning, she dressed in her best ruffled slip, picked up her tiny purse with less than 25 cents in it and headed downtown—alone and barefoot—to go and buy herself some new shoes.

When my mother saw that Barbara was gone, she flew into a panic. She looked all over the yard, then ran to the grocery store to get our father. Dad, still in his grocer's apron, searched frantically with Mom. They went house to house and were about to involve our relatives and neighbors in a wider search when a police car rolled up. And there was Barbara, standing up in the front seat between the policemen, her arms stretched across the seat back as if she were hugging them.

The shoe store owner had called the police, and Barbara directed the officers to our house. Barbara couldn't understand what the big deal was, but Mom and Dad were so happy to see her alive and well they snapped a picture of us.

PEGGY FRIESEN · STOCKTON, CA

Revealing Her True Self

Young writer sees the woman she will become.

When I turned 11 in 1982, I received a truly memorable gift—my first real diary, with a lock and key. The cover had "Diary" emblazoned in huge letters and it was decorated with a Snoopy. It was a gift from my classmate Dan and his older sister Denise, who both loved the Peanuts gang. It was the kind of gift my parents would not buy for me. As the only child of frugal, first-generation immigrants, I was overprotected, but because this book came from friends, it was allowed.

In fifth grade creative writing at Villa Victoria Academy, I often got so absorbed in my writing that I wouldn't hear the bell. Yet as the proud owner of a real diary, I was so excited that I didn't know what to write— my first bout of writer's block. The book stayed beneath my bed for months. It was only when I got chickenpox and was home from school for three weeks that I wrote my first entry.

Oct. 11, 1982: "I am home, I cannot go to school because I am sick. I miss my friends and creative writing. Oh, no!"

In 1984, I turned 13 and I felt things changing. Out came the diary and soon I was writing in it daily.

Dec. 6, 1984: "What can I do? I'm upset that my best friends don't get along with each other and don't want to sit at the same lunch table! I can't split myself in half."

Looking back, I chuckle at my music, TV and sartorial choices: Menudo, Duran Duran, *The Brady Bunch*, Scooby-Doo, Gitano and Sergio Valente jeans, Benetton sweaters. But I'm amazed by my understanding of who I was inside.

April 27, 1985: "I'm good at writing, piano, reading aloud (which used to come easily for me, but now I stutter more than before), Spanish class. I'm not good at gym (but I do enjoy walking and dancing to my own choreography). I'm shy but I talk a lot when I'm with people who make me laugh.

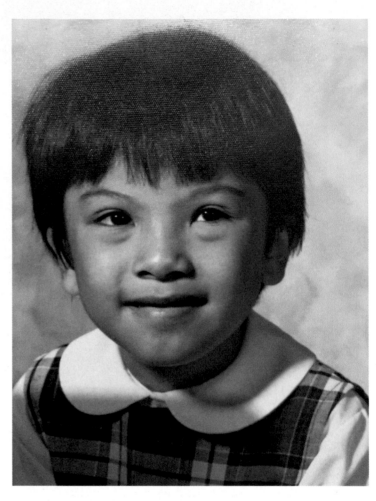

Leonora's views of teenage life were surprisingly grown-up.

I like science but I'm afraid of lab work and setting things on fire. I get crushes on good-looking boys quite easily and intensely but I'm not good at flirting because I get tongue-tied and nervous and can't think of anything to say even though I'm a chatterbox. Why does small talk have to be about small things? I want to talk about the galaxy and constellations."

Today, I'm in awe of my younger self. And I see that my appreciation for fine paper started then, as did the special joy of writing in cursive.

LEONORA RITA V. OBED
WEST TRENTON, NJ

His bike fitted with a buggy, Kent gives his friend Rich Babin a ride. Spunky gets in on the action, too.

Traveling Companions

Grandma and Spunky the dog were always up for an adventure.

After the Great Depression, Grandma Helen Dunbar moved from South Dakota to a ranch in northern Idaho. By the time I was a little boy there, she was a full-time grandma, able to spend time with me and Spunky, a tan puppy who was so very small when I got him that he fit in my 10-year-old hands.

With Spunky tucked in my coat, I rode my bike to Grandma's house to watch as she made noodles. She laid them everywhere to dry—on countertops, on the bed and on sheets on the floor. It was always all we could do to keep Spunky out of the noodles.

From the time I was 12, in 1965, we all spent the summers in a trailer in the woods to be closer to my stepdad's logging work. I put up a large canvas tent for myself, and Grandma sawed boards for the floor. She loved to fish near camp, staying out so long that the fish had to give up and bite her hook.

Spunky came along when I biked to the country store in Murray, several miles from camp. On one trip we found a motherless baby skunk—of course,

I brought it home. The next day, we found more babies to bring to Grandma, who fed them with an eyedropper.

Years later, I spent summers in the woods while working for the U.S. Forest Service and earning money for college. Grandma still liked to fish, and on a hike with me to a mountain lake, she went up the steep grade like a youngster.

Despite her love of fishing, Grandma never learned to swim, and I always worried that she would fall into a river. The year she turned 64, Grandma died in an accident that landed her car in the river. She and Spunky were on their way to spend a week in the woods; I was set to join them after work. Spunky survived—carried downstream, he climbed out of the river and walked to the highway, where I found him.

I was lucky to grow up with a best dog and a best grandma—the time that I had with them made me who I am.

KENT KRONE · DIXON, MT

SCHOOL DAYS

STAR MATERIAL

Our dance teachers, Joe and Grace O'Donnell, created *The Star Parade*, a radio show that aired on *WARM* in Scranton in 1940. I got to sing the opening song every week—I still remember every word. I'm second from the right in the white sweater.

ELIZABETH HOLLENBACK NEARY
SHREWSBURY, PA

JUNIOR HIGH OPPOSITES ATTRACT

Shy, quiet Roxie (right) and I met in seventh grade, and we hit it off immediately. I might've been a bad influence on her!

TINA BERKEN BEMENT · DOUGLAS, IA

MAKING THE TRIP

My grandfather Guy Thompson entered second grade in the new school in Melvin, IL, in 1904. My brother Eric was in the last second-grade class in that school in the early '60s. Grandpa came along when Eric and his classmates bagged up their supplies in brown paper grocery sacks to walk to the new school.

LISA KRALL · DEWEY, IL

MARCHING RIGHT ALONG
As one of our high school band's majorettes, I kept the beat in style.
SANDI WALLACE · TAMPA, FL

Blinded by Science

Chemistry nerds were in their element—until they got an unexpected reaction.

As teenagers, my friend Peter and I spent our time experimenting and tinkering. Peter's father was a top chemist for Mobil, making Peter a natural partner when we started our own chemical laboratory in 1963.

Every weekend, we took the bus to Arthur H. Thomas Co. in Philadelphia, Pennsylvania, to buy laboratory equipment. Using tips earned from delivering newspapers, we acquired beakers, test tubes and a Bunsen burner, and soon we had a well-equipped chemistry lab—equal to the one in our high school, at least.

All we needed to acquire were some chemicals for our experiments.

With an ink pad and lettering stamp, we used some of my father's stationery to make letterhead for Car-Pet (which was a combination of my last name, Carson, and Peter's name) Chemical Laboratories, and we listed my home address in Woodbury, New Jersey.

Every day during our school lunch hour, we wrote letters to chemical companies we'd found in professional journals and industry publications. We contacted Allied Chemical, Rohm and Haas Chemicals, Dow, Hercules and DuPont, and we

A high school chem classroom, such as the one on page 18, was the model for the lab that Alex, left, and Peter set up in the Carsons' basement.

My mother was pleased Peter and I were doing something "educational."

requested carbon, sulfur, nitric acid, potassium and anything else we could get for free. Some of these chemicals were relatively safe, but others were downright hazardous.

Two weeks passed, and we were utterly surprised to see a Mack truck on our street, breaking off tree limbs and avoiding parked cars as it approached my house. The 6-pound shipment from Armour Industrial Chemical Co. was labeled Fragile Liquid. More shipments arrived, some by mail, all marked with warning labels.

School ended, and we went swimming most days, so some shipments were dropped at the neighbors. My mother was pleased Peter and I were doing something "educational," but the neighbors looked suspiciously at the hazard labels when they brought the boxes over.

One day while my father was at work, he got a call from the FBI. Peter and I had requested a free sample of a rocket fuel from Rohm and Haas in Philadelphia, completely unaware that it was a top secret formulation for the federal government. Fortunately, the FBI deemed us not to be a threat

and took no further action on our case. Dad was furious and told Peter's family about our pastime. Car-Pet Chemical Labs was forced out of business, and Peter and I had to dismantle the lab.

Rather than letting all those chemicals go to waste, Peter and I decided to make one last concoction: urea formaldehyde resin, which we'd heard about from Peter's dad. In our basement lab, we combined the chemicals, with all going well until a thick white cloud of noxious smoke erupted from the Florence flask we were heating. The irritating chemical fumes drove everyone out of the house, including my mother.

Luckily no one was injured, but with the fumes lingering, my mother ordered us to dig a hole in the backyard and throw all the chemicals in, ending our experiment for good.

I don't know if Peter had a career that involved chemistry. I worked in law enforcement, but I'm grateful for that time we had to busy ourselves with teenage experimentation gone a little haywire.

ALEXANDER G. CARSON · MAGNOLIA, DE

Dusty won fans everywhere Sally took him in 1954.

Market Day is a Hard Sell

4-H friend runs rings around girl's heart.

Growing up in northwest Kansas in 1954, I was a not-very-avid 4-H'er and had trouble choosing a project. But I liked animals, and when Dad brought home a lamb that had been rejected by its mother, I fell in love. I fed the darling ball of fleece on a strict schedule, and soon Dusty was following me everywhere.

As 4-H'ers do, I paid for the project with a loan from the bank—the staggering sum of $25. I knew from watching my three older siblings excel in 4-H that projects should not become pets, but I told myself that they had never had a lamb!

I entered Dusty in a Fourth of July parade in nearby Palco, Kansas. He had many admirers as I proudly led him—fresh from a bath that turned our bathroom into a slimy, muddy, reeking mess. Midway down Main Street, Dusty skidded to a halt, ignoring my pleas as the rest of the parade moved around us. Dad had to lift him into the car. Only a late-afternoon call from the parade director telling me that I had won first place in the pet division got the misbehaving Dusty back in my good graces.

At the 4-H fair, Dusty was the darling of the barn. I'd agreed to sell him to repay my loan, but I clung to the hope that my parents would bail me out. In the ring, instead of focusing on showing him off to potential buyers, I searched the tearful faces of his fans lining the sale barn ring and tried not to cry myself.

When the auctioneer banged his gavel and boomed "Sold!" I dropped the leash. I ran sobbing to my dad as Dusty was led away.

Just when I was certain life as I knew it was over, Dad introduced me to a tall man—Dusty's buyer. He leaned down and said, "Don't worry, Sally. I bought your Dusty for my four grandchildren. He's all they've talked about this week, and they begged me to rescue him."

That wonderful reassurance was music to a 10-year-old girl's ears.

SALLY PHIFER · SANDY, OR

Snagging the Past

Old mitt holds fond memories.

When I came across my old baseball mitt in a wooden crate recently, my mind flashed back to my boyhood and endless summer days in Ohio.

Suddenly, Dad was teaching me how to scoop up ground balls, and I felt again the sting of a wild hop that I stopped with my face instead of the mitt. I threw the mitt down in frustration, but Dad taught me not to give up if life takes a bad bounce. I remembered the smell of mown grass and chatter of my Little League teammates as I chased a fly ball that, to my surprise, somehow found its way into my mitt. Later, I brought that mitt to my first major league baseball game in Cincinnati, hoping to catch a foul ball in the stands—no such luck. I still have hopes of getting a foul ball someday.

When we moved from Ohio to Illinois, I met an Irish lad named Patrick Sullivan, and we spent many an afternoon tossing a scuffed-up baseball back and forth as we talked about girls, school, sports, and our hopes and dreams. I'm not sure where Patrick is these days, but I sure wish we could catch up.

My trusty baseball glove followed me to college, where I was team MVP in an intramural tournament. I helped us win a big game with two doubles, and I snagged the final out with my mitt. Once again, no one was more surprised than me.

DAVID WARREN · MIAMISBURG, OH

FOCUS ON: BASEBALL MITT

It's difficult to date David's mitt because he and his dad found it at a yard sale; it still bears the name of the previous owner handwritten on the side. It's a Rawlings, probably mid-to-late '60s, with a padded palm called an Edge-U-Cated heel. Gloves of this vintage appear on resale sites for around $30, but some can sell for far more. Condition is key, as is model or style. Mint mitts are collectors' prizes; well-loved gloves usually are destined for backyard games.

David's glove saw him through Little League. In this 1971 team shot he's second from left, with his mitt resting on his left knee.

Leave a Paper, Take a Puppy

Farm-route carrier gets unusual tip.

Back in Council Bluffs, Iowa, in the 1940s, I was 10-going-on-11 and wanting a paper route. The manager of The Daily Nonpareil lived close to my friend. If he was around when I was at my friend's house, I'd bug him to give me a route. He kept saying no, because I had to be 12. Finally, my constant bothering paid off. The manager assigned me route No. 64, which was in my neighborhood.

I didn't have a bike, so I walked the route, which included a few farms. Early on, a customer's farm dogs had a litter of puppies. Every day the woman would tell me that I needed a dog. Eventually I broke down and took one. I named her Boots.

I had a big route—117 papers—and I threw the rolled-up papers onto the porch as I went by. One day, the wind blew the paper onto the roof of a house. I didn't have extras, so I left. I got 50 yards away before I felt a hand on my shoulder—my displeased customer. "You little blankety-blank, get up on that roof and get that paper!"

I made $4.50 a week. If someone complained, you were docked 15 cents. The paper was thin on weekdays, and a truck would drop off the bundle at a store near my house. But on Sundays, I had to go to the printing plant in town to pick them up. I'd fill my burlap bag and then catch a streetcar back to my route to start delivering.

And Boots? She followed me everywhere, right up until I joined the Air Force, when my mother took her in. We renewed our bond when I was stationed at Offutt Air Force Base in Nebraska. Boots lived for 17 years—I am 88 now and still remember her. I loved that dog.

EARL KENNEDY · DOVER, AR

Chuck Johnson devises an efficient method for lugging his bundle of *Minneapolis Tribunes* in 1975.

Sitrin siblings Joyce, 5, and Charles, 4, stand on the snowy porch of the family home in Utica, NY, in 1947.

Escape from the Chains of Winter

Transplant finds cold months in the South are a breeze.

———

My hometown, Utica, New York, is smack in the middle of the state's Mohawk Valley. Winter lasts a full six months, during which the valley is blessed with several feet of snow. As a kid, I took it in stride.

The season started when Dad took our car to the garage to have chains put on the tires. With those, you could drive practically anywhere, no matter how heavy the snowfall.

On Saturdays we hiked with friends to the great sledding hill in the town park, and spent the day trudging up and sliding madly down. We each had our own sled, a wooden one you could steer. Teenagers preferred the four-seater toboggans, which generally dumped the riders in a heap when they hit the big bumps.

School never closed for a snow day: After one ice storm, children had to crawl across slippery sidewalks on their way to school. We looked down on the fainthearted children from milder climes, and respected the hardy Green Bay Packers fans who sat cheering on their team through whiteouts.

When a more serious snowstorm would descend, all of us—Mom, Dad and we three children—took turns shoveling in two-hour shifts to keep the porch, sidewalks and driveway clear.

After college I wound up moving as far south as Massachusetts, which I considered soft when it came to dealing with snow. I now live in Virginia and have become soft myself.

Here, the schools close and people stock up on water when 2 inches of snow are predicted. Snowplow crews wait until the "storm" is over before attempting to clear the streets. My younger Utica self would have found it all very amusing.

JOYCE LEE MALCOLM · ALEXANDRIA, VA

YOU HAD ME AT JELL-O

Gelatin desserts have been popular in the United States since Thomas Jefferson's banquets, and their appeal endures today.

1956 »

An Indulgent Treat

Jell-O takes a hedonistic approach in this ad, promising "deep, dark and delicious desserts" that look as decadent as they do colorful.

NEW! NEW! NEW!

For deep, dark and delicious desserts

BLACK CHERRY   BLACK RASPBERRY   GRAPE

3 NEW JELL-O FLAVORS

We've captured **three** wonderful *new* flavors to bring a new kind of dessert variety to your table!

They're deep, dark and delicious delights that imitate to perfection the exciting taste of sun-ripened black raspberries, the darkest, juiciest cherries on the tree, and plump, deep-purple Concord grapes.

For extra-colorful, extra-flavorful new desserts, try all three: *Imitation Black Raspberry, Imitation Black Cherry* and *Imitation Grape* flavors.

JELL-O New!
IMITATION BLACK CHERRY FLAVOR

New JELL-O
IMITATION BLACK RASPBERRY FLAVOR

JELL-O NEW
IMITATION GRAPE FLAVOR

JELL-O IS A REGISTERED TRADE-MARK OF GENERAL FOODS CORPORATION

Real Raspberries 35 to 50 of them are used for the flavor of a single package of Royal Raspberry Gelatin

ROYAL
Quick Setting GELATIN DESSERT
RASPBERRY FLAVOR

« 1936

No Knock-Offs Here!

In contrast to the "imitation" flavors of some brands, real raspberries—"35 to 50 of them" per package, in fact— were touted proudly in this Royal promotion.

Strawberry Jell-O

"Bringing Home a Basketful of Happiness."

MOTHERS have learned that the perfectly healthy child is the child who eats with a relish, that it is inexpedient to provide children with food which is repugnant to them, and that a simple, palatable dessert is both refreshing and wholesome for the child with a small appetite. They have learned, too, that rather than discourage a liking for sweets in their children, it is far better to provide the right sort of sweet dishes, and to encourage the child to eat and enjoy them.

The American Offices and Factory of the Genesee Pure Food Company are at Le Roy, N. Y., in the famous Genesee Valley Country. The Offices and Factory of the Genesee Pure Food Company of Canada, Ltd., are at Bridgeburg, Ontario, on the Niagara River

« 1922

A Basketful of Happiness
In a time before low-calorie options like sugar-free Jell-O were available, the company urged parents to let kids indulge in the syrupy snack.

1963 »

Dessert is the Best Medicine
As adding vitamin supplements to food products became a widely used tactic to boost sales, Royal first added in vitamin C to its gelatin desserts in 1955.

VITAMIN C ADDED

Royal gelatin dessert

LIME FLAVOR

REGULAR OR NEW FAMILY-SIZE PACKAGE

Royal is the only gelatin that gives you fresh fruit flavor plus fresh fruit Vitamin C. Reach for **Royal**
the tender – textured gelatin

Room and Board for the Winter

Family learns there's no reason
to be in a flap about a surprise guest.

———

December 1952 in Whitewater, Wisconsin, was bitterly cold. As a curious 7-year-old, I was in suspense when my father arrived home from work with something bundled in his jacket. "Guess what I have," he said.

He slowly unwrapped the jacket to reveal a stiff screech-owl. He'd found the frozen bird on the hood of his car when he left work and speculated that it had flown into the windshield.

Dad thought it might be alive and wanted to let it warm up. My mother agreed to let the bird stay overnight, so Dad and I took it to the basement and carefully laid it near our coal furnace.

I was the first one into the kitchen the next morning for a bowl of cereal. I looked up from

Randall enjoyed the family's unusual pest controller, an owl like the one at left, sheltering in the basement in 1952.

of the basement. Soon Dad and I were laughing too hard to continue the chase, and we realized there was no way we could evict the owl if it wanted to stay.

As Dad left for work and I went to school, Mom wondered how she was supposed to do the laundry, since the washing machine was located in the basement. She quickly realized that my 2-year-old brother's fascination with the wild bird kept him busy. In turn, the owl tolerated our presence, and Mom resigned herself to having it in the house until Dad could catch it when it became weak from hunger.

But that never happened.

The coal door, which didn't seal well, allowed mice into the basement. The owl had been in our basement for just a few days when Dad showed me an owl pellet, the tidy nugget of indigestible parts that an owl regurgitates.

Over the winter, we found these regularly, and the owl became so fat Dad might have easily caught it. But, by that time, we liked the natural rodent control, and I enjoyed showing my friends the owl that lived in my basement and explaining its eating habits.

Spring came late that year, and within a few weeks we found no more owl pellets. Warmer weather meant that mice no longer took shelter in our basement and that the owl had run out of its once-abundant food. We opened the back door and were prepared to harass the bird for as long as it took to get it outside.

But the owl knew it was time to leave: With a single wave of the broom, Dad chased it up the stairs, out the door and into the tall pear tree in our backyard. We observed the owl around the neighborhood for a few more days and then the bird was gone.

We felt a sense of loss. The owl had given us hours of entertainment in repayment for its rescue. We took comfort knowing it was free and healthy, if a bit overweight.

Almost 70 years have passed. I recently asked Mom if she remembers that owl, and she smiled broadly. My brother remembers, too. And since that cold December evening in 1952, I cannot hear the words "guess what I have" without remembering my father unwrapping a frozen screech-owl.

RANDALL SCHAEFER · HASTINGS, MI

peering into the box for the prize and was face to face with the screech-owl. It perched on the sugar bowl as if waiting for its breakfast.

I hurried to tell my parents that the owl was alive and sitting at the kitchen table. Mom didn't like that it was in the kitchen, and she wanted it out of the house.

Dad instructed me to open the back door while he shooed the owl toward me. I heard the flapping of wings, but before I could direct its flight outside, the owl spun away from the frigid air coming in the door and zipped past me, down the stairs into the shelter of the warm basement.

Perched in the space above the beams, the owl was safely beyond our reach. We tried driving it out with a broom, but it calmly flew to the far side

Belle enjoys sweet, loving attention from Curtis, Deanna and Aunt Eunice.

Our Southern Belle

Loyal hunting dog would not be moved from her post.

———

We lived in the mountains of western North Carolina, in an area known as Fruitland for the apple trees that grew there. I was born in 1943 and was close to my older brother, Curtis, in age and loyal friendship, with a little sibling rivalry thrown in.

My father, a carpenter, built our house. A porch wrapped around the front and side of the rock-faced structure. Past the soft green lawn, the property was surrounded by forest.

During the hot summers, Curtis and I spent our days outside with old Belle, our father's bird dog. We loved to play on a large pile of rocks that was left over from the construction of the house.

One morning when we went outside to play, we couldn't find Belle. We called, but she didn't come.

Finally, we found her standing near the pile of rocks that was our playground.

As we approached the rocks, Belle growled at us. Surprised, we went back to the house and told our mother about Belle's unusual behavior. Mother came out to see for herself, but when she tried to come close to Belle, the dog again gave a warning growl. Our mother told us to stay away. All day, Belle stood without food or water by the rocks.

When our father returned, he went to check on Belle. On seeing him, Belle assumed the hunting stance, with her front paw raised and curled. There in the rocks, where Belle's nose was pointing, my father found a large copperhead snake. Our beloved Belle had kept us safe.

DEANNA HEUER · WAYNESBORO, PA

PUPPY TAKES HIS PLACE AS TOP DOG ON THE FARM

OUR ST. BERNARD, YANTO, was a clumsy puppy with big feet, but he grew quickly into an agile dog.

My mother, Mary, a dog lover, had a special bond with him. When she gathered eggs, she closed the door of the coop so Yanto couldn't enter, but one day he pushed inside, panicking the hens and knocking over the half-filled pail of eggs, breaking most of them.

He loved to ride on the wagon behind the tractor. He put his front feet on the wagon and barked for someone to give his 180-pound behind a boost. He sat on the bales, climbing to the top as each layer was added. When the loaded wagon returned to the farmyard, Yanto sat high up in the sky. He was a wonderful, entertaining part of our life.

MALCOLM DIRKSEN · TWIN BROOKS, SD

BRINGING HOME BUTTONS

When I saw Buttons at the pet store in 1946, I fell in love. I bought him with the money I'd saved from my first Holy Communion. Buttons was an excellent pet and, to this day, I've never been without a dog in my life.

JOHN CISLER · SARASOTA, FL

When Mary saw an ad for puppies, she couldn't resist seeing them for herself. She came home with Yanto, a registered St. Bernard.

THE WATCHFUL EYE OF JEEP

Jeep was a young Canada goose that my Grandma Hopp gave me as a pet. He served as a "watch goose," which meant squawking to bring my parents running when, as a 3-year-old, I learned to unlatch the gate and run out to the street. We were friends until Jeep was no longer a good playmate.

CHUCK RANG · NEW RICHMOND, WI

John and Wynne took piano lessons with Mrs. C from 1948 to '53.

Middle C to Rachmaninoff

Mrs. C taught a classical education.

Piano lessons are no longer thought of as a necessary part of a proper education, but in the 1950s most children took piano lessons. For my brother, John, and me, lessons started a half-hour after school ended. It was a mile-long walk from our elementary school to the home of Mrs. Helen Nancy Congdon in Tacoma, Washington. There was no dawdling.

Part of Mrs. C's front porch was converted into a tiny waiting room, with literature about the lives of classical pianists and a smattering of children's magazines. Mrs. C also gave us copies of *Keyboard Jr.*, a monthly magazine about other kids playing the piano.

When the previous student finished, a buzzer let me know she was ready for me. I maneuvered around Seymour, a little yapping poodle, and took my place on the ebony bench—no slouching— while Mrs. C sat by my right hand, sipping her ever-present cup of tea. If our performance was satisfactory, she pasted a red star on the music. Mistakes were circled in red.

Two baby grand pianos were squeezed into her living room for duets. Mrs. C played the thump thump of the secondo on one, while I tried to master the melody on the other.

Neither John nor I had an ear for music—we memorized our pieces note by note on our Baldwin Acrosonic spinet for the May recitals, where we all dressed up and received polite applause from the parents. I worked very diligently to play Rachmaninoff's Prelude in C Sharp Minor as a high school senior.

Piano lessons gave me an admiration for classical music and, although my playing ability didn't stick, I still remember those first three lofty chords from the prelude.

WYNNE CROMBIE · NICHOLASVILLE, KY

Winter's Way

My brothers and I explore the Hocking Hills near Logan, Ohio, with our
dad in 1958. I always look on this photo as a father leading his sons along
the path of life. It has a powerful message for me.

GREG GROOM · COLUMBUS, OH

CHAPTER 2

ALL IN THE FAMILY

Brothers, sisters, parents and pets—they always made us smile, and there was no obstacle too large for everyone to weather together.

MAY · 5 5

Fall of '76

My children Eric, in plaid, and Barb, in gingham shirt and cutoffs,
look like the cartoon characters Li'l Abner and Daisy Mae in this
bright photo taken on a warm autumn day in the mid-1970s.

J. BIRNEY DIBBLE · EAU CLAIRE, WI

Moonlighting in the Strawberry Patch

Gardening side job was a labor of love.

———

My mom's parents immigrated from Cenkov, a town in what is now Czechia. Frantisek "Frank" Hruska and Marie Vokurka had traveled separately to Milwaukee, Wisconsin, and met in the local Bohemian Hall. They kept company for a time, and eventually Frank persuaded 22-year-old Marie to join him and his brothers for a Fourth of July celebration. During the visit—the family story goes—Frank's brothers conspired to get the couple married. My mom, Otillia Ann, was born one year later, on July 4, 1907.

Grandpa worked in Milwaukee as a harness maker, but within a few years his brothers urged him to move his family to Menominee, Michigan. Signal Electric Manufacturing Co. had opened a new factory there to produce crystal radio sets, which were just becoming popular.

Frank Hruska assembled radios by day.

The money Grandpa made from his strawberry plots more than doubled his factory earnings.

Frank's brothers helped him build a house on a property of several acres. Grandpa was an excellent gardener, and he planted grass, vegetables, fruit trees and shade trees on his new land. Grandma worked hard, too, caring for the children, canning and tending to the cow, chickens and geese. But with my mom and her two siblings rapidly growing, Grandpa felt they needed more. He wanted to expand his earnings for a better life.

After studying the possibilities for cash crops, Grandpa bought his first 50 strawberry plants. He already sold extra produce from his garden to local grocers, and he soon began filling orders for strawberries, too. Starting before sunrise each morning during strawberry season, Mom and her siblings, Mary and George, joined Grandpa in the rows picking and boxing the sweet fruit. Mom remembered the intense flavor of the strawberries, and always claimed there was no comparison

between the big, sweet berries that grew on Grandpa's plots and the bland ones that were sold in grocery stores.

The berries grew in such abundance that the workers could fill a quart box from every 6 inches of row, and—during the height of the season— they'd fill 50 crates each and every day. Grandpa would then deliver his fruit to the local grocers before starting his shift at the factory. The hard work paid off: The money that Grandpa made from his strawberry plots more than doubled his factory earnings.

After a very long day in the factory, Grandpa would work out in the garden until dark. Long after his strawberry business ended, Grandpa continued to garden—he was still at it in the 1960s when he was 80.

FRANK SUETHOLZ · RACINE, WI

Sham Always Made it Through

Son recalls his father's challenges in tough times.

One of 10 children, my father, named John Michael but known as Sham for his Irish ancestry, grew up on a farm outside of Dunlap, Iowa.

He looked forward to Saturdays, when he got a quarter to shoot pool in town. Later, my father taught me many things amid the hard work of raising his family—how to shave, drive a car, play pinochle. Included in the list was how to shoot a fair game of pool.

My parents, Sham and Thelma Jean, married in November 1928, shortly before the stock market collapsed.

During the Great Depression, my father was among the millions of jobless working-class men who stood in bread lines to feed their families, but my parents never talked about being so desperate. Dad later found work through President Franklin D. Roosevelt's New Deal and the Works Progress Administration (WPA).

My sister Bonnie Jean was born in 1934. By then, our dad had a job at the Ford Motor Co. plant in Kansas City, Missouri. Using a heavy grinder, he smoothed out small dents in new models that rolled along the assembly line.

He earned 50 cents an hour until he lost his job when the company let several employees go and hired people who agreed to work for less. The union sued after Dad and others were targeted for picketing the plant. My father decided that it was time for us to move on.

In 1940, we arrived in California, where Dad got a job at a Lockheed Corp. plant in Burbank. He purchased our first house, a nearly new two-bedroom tract home, for $3,400—$50 down and monthly installments of $31.

The Hawns pose in front of their new home in California in 1941, far left, and Bonnie and Jack go for a spin in Richmond, VA, in 1939.

That day attending the game with me was one of the happiest of his life. And it is one of my favorite memories of our time together.

He sold it seven years later for $10,500.

In the early 1940s, we received more excellent news: The union had won its lawsuit against Ford. Dad used his portion of the settlement to purchase the only brand-new car he ever owned. (It was a Chevrolet.)

Finally, at age 43, my father found his calling when he bought a small tavern in rural Oak View, California, about 4 miles from Ojai. The Shamrock Inn opened on St. Patrick's Day in 1947.

He loved owning the tavern, and by then he'd earned some simple pleasures. A sports fanatic, Dad was thrilled when I became a sports writer for a Hollywood newspaper and got him tickets to various events.

Unforgettable was the night of Oct. 21, 1953, when we attended a football game between Notre Dame and the University of Southern California.

We enjoyed an early dinner at Julie's, a popular sports bar located in the shadow of the Los Angeles Memorial Coliseum. While we were there, we watched a world middleweight boxing championship on the bar's TV.

Someone passed a hat with slips numbered from 1 to 15—whoever had the number of the round when the fight ended would win $75. Dad was glad to draw a low number because oddsmakers favored Randy Turpin, a ferocious puncher, over Carl "Bobo" Olson, who was not regarded as a heavy hitter. I got 15.

"Trade you, Dad," I said. "This could go the distance, you know."

Dad said no—he wasn't born yesterday. All the same, he should have accepted my offer. Bobo Olson took the title with a 15-round decision. It was the only time I can remember beating my father at anything.

On the way to the Coliseum, Dad had to stop to catch his breath. He recovered, but I was worried about him for the rest of the night. As he gingerly stepped out of the elevator on the way to the press box, someone behind him whispered, "It's like he's walking on eggs."

I'm sure Dad heard, but it didn't matter. He took his seat in front of the large window eager to cheer for the Fighting Irish.

Dad passed away a few months later, but that day attending the game with me was one of the happiest of his life. And it is one of my favorite memories of our time together.

JACK HAWN · SUN CITY WEST, AZ

David makes an entrance as Gleason.

Putting a Spin on Jackie Gleason Reruns

Dad's photography studio was the setting for producing kids' version of favorite show.

My little brother, David, and I were crazy about Jackie Gleason in the early 1960s. We never missed *Jackie Gleason: American Scene Magazine* on Saturday nights. Maybe it was because our parents liked *The Honeymooners* so much that we became such dedicated fans.

My father owned a photography studio and once a week, my brother and I spent the day with him there. While he developed pictures in the darkroom, we played in the studio where there were big cameras, lighting umbrellas and all sorts of other photography equipment. Floor-length curtains, which were a background for studio

Left: A fake plastic belly adds the final touch to David's wardrobe. Top: He holds up a picture he took of the TV screen when *American Scene Magazine* came on.

portraits, became the backdrop for our imaginary stage, where we acted out whole shows by heart.

We played all the different characters from the skits we'd seen on Saturday nights. David pretended that he was announcer Johnny Olson, introducing Sammy Spear and His Orchestra. Then he appeared as Jackie Gleason himself, imitating his trademark "And awaaay we go!"

My father, knowing how much my brother loved pretending to be Gleason, surprised him with a fake belly made of molded plastic. David was elated: It was the finishing touch to his costume as he came from behind the curtain exclaiming "How sweeeet it is!"

Our favorite sketch was Joe the Bartender. David wore a white shirt, parted his hair in the middle and stood behind a table to simulate the bar.

He pretended to read *The American Scene* magazine or sang "My Gal Sal," and then looked

up to talk to the imaginary Mr. Dennehy. A few minutes later, I entered, wearing a hat like Frank Fontaine wore, doing my best impression of Crazy Guggenheim. I waved and said, "Hiya, Joe! Hiya, Mr. Dennehy!"

When I was 9 and David was 6, our father surprised us with tickets to Gleason's live show in New York City. We drove from New Jersey through the Lincoln Tunnel, cheering when we passed the painted line on the tunnel wall showing that we were now in New York.

At CBS Studio 50, we sat close to the stage, watching the June Taylor Dancers make their kaleidoscope formations. Between the skits, Johnny Olson came out on stage, telling the audience to applaud. Of course, David and I clapped as hard as we could.

NANCY JOHNSON KRAMPERT · SELINSGROVE, PA

DRESSED ALIKE

» CUT FROM THE SAME CLOTH

Dressing us in matching frocks with turquoise belts in 1962 was as close as our mom, Alvena, got to her wish of having twins.

JAN HINES
MANSFIELD, OH

⌄ HERE COME THE BRIDES

Granddaughter Faren Culp and I modeled wedding attire for a Mother's Day program at church in 1994.

JUDY GREENMAN
HUTCHINSON, MN

THREE'S A CHARM

Here is a picture of my three children and me with look-alike clothing.

KATHRYN WORCESTER
BRAINERD, MINNESOTA

PATTERNED AFTER MOM
My mother, Wilma Hawes Connely, and I modeled the blue and white striped Easter dresses she made for us in 1962. I was 6.
CONNIE CONNELY · TULSA, OK

In 1974, Jacklyn, 16, stands behind Ingrid, Caroline and their dad, Jack, at the Brighton Resort, about 30 miles south of Salt Lake City.

The Day Went Downhill

Dad pulled everyone into a new family activity.

Lehi, Utah, where my family moved in 1974, is surrounded by mountains. My father, Jack Hansen, had skied once, in Idaho, and he wanted us all to learn. It was easy, he said, and he got skis, boots and poles for me, my sisters Ingrid and Caroline, and my stepmother. We scrambled around for suitable clothes; I wore jeans.

Dad showed us how to clamp the skis to our boots, and how they would release if we fell. This was our only instruction. We stood as the ski lift came quickly behind us, bending our knees so we wouldn't get knocked over.

The ride on the lift felt like flying, but as I neared the top, the ground dropped away. "Jump, and bend your knees!" my father yelled.

I wanted to stay on the lift, but I jumped, falling and losing my skis. Dad got me to my feet and pointed down the hill. Balancing on two slippery pieces of wood, I sped off, stopping only when I fell and lost my skis again.

When I got to the bottom, I was ready to quit. But Dad insisted I get back on the lift.

I soon developed a tiresome and not-very-fun pattern: going too fast, falling, watching my skis detach from my boots, getting up and reattaching the skis. Repeat.

After our last run, my sisters showed me the snowplow technique they'd taught themselves: Pointing the front ends of the skis in toward each other slowed the descent.

We skied a few more times that year, and I learned to snowplow and turn corners without falling, but I never learned to like skiing.

JACKLYN ANDERSON · GLENDALE, AZ

What'll It Be, Dad?

She was always careful not to spill a drop.

Nothing pleased me more than when my dad called to me from the den where he was watching TV, "Hey, Rob. Make me a gin and tonic, would ya?"

This may seem like questionable parenting of an 8-year-old, but I loved the feeling of importance in performing this special chore. And he always had just one.

I'd run to the barrel-shaped liquor cabinet. Its brass latch was heavy, and the door was hard to open. Inside, it was dark and sweet-smelling. There was no telling how old the schnapps, bourbon and vodka were; most of the liquors were from the days when Mom and Dad entertained before they had children.

I liked the purple velvet bag that held one bottle, and the tag hanging around the neck of another. I put it on my arm, pretending it was a bracelet. Best of all were the bone-shaped swizzle sticks, topped with skulls and gemstone eyes.

I carried the big bottle of cheap gin to the kitchen, where I climbed onto a stool. I put ice cubes in Dad's special highball glass, then gin—two fingers—then tonic. He didn't bother with limes. One final step—"Give it a swizzle!"

Who knows how long I spent mixing to get his drink just right, but my father was patient and never made me feel rushed. He took a sip. With pinkie finger extended, he looked at me and declared, "Poifect!"

Once when Mom happened upon this ritual, she looked disapprovingly at Dad and said, "Duff!"

Without batting an eye he replied, "Well, I didn't tell her to drink it, Ida." One time he did end up letting me taste the drink, with its pungent sting of juniper.

Once was enough.

ROBIN DUFFY · CHAPEL HILL, NC

Robin loved the every-once-in-a-while ritual of fixing her dad, Don, a drink.

Glenda's success at tennis was a point of pride in her family's letters to her. Here she readies a killer backhand shot in 1975.

Cora told her granddaughter of daily happenings. Grandfather Henry preferred to draw his hellos.

Lifeline via the P.O. Box

When she left for college in 1972, it was the first time she'd been away from home.

Even though College of the Ozarks was only a four-hour drive from my family in Chamois, Missouri, I was quite homesick in 1972—I'd never been away from home. Our dorm didn't have phones in the rooms. Communication from family came to me at P.O. Box 469, Point Lookout, MO.

I would receive letters, cards and, occasionally, a pink slip that told me I had a large package. The post office became an important link to my family.

Not only did I get letters from Mom and Dad, I received letters from my grandmothers, aunts, cousins and, later, from my brother in the military. I always wrote a letter back. It's a wonder I had any time to attend classes and study.

My grandmother Cora Walker would write every week, describing everyday events and saying that it must make for boring reading. Those are the very things I treasure when I reread her letters now.

My grandfather Henry wasn't much for writing—he left that to my grandmother—but he did like to draw. When I wrote to them about a tennis tournament I had entered, my grandfather already decided the outcome: He sent me a drawing of me winning. (In fact, I did win the championship.)

My grandparents would send me $5 or $10 for birthdays or just in case I needed spending money. I could always tell when their letter had cash inside because the bill was wrapped in foil. I suppose they were trying to "foil" anyone trying to see through the envelope.

I saved every letter I received. Later, I learned that my mother and grandmother did the same with my letters to them. I have four years' worth of saved letters in binders. Together they form a time capsule of my college years.

GLENDA FERGUSON · PAOLI, IN

OUTDOOR ADVENTURES

ICY CONDITIONS

We always loved it when our parents told us to get our ice skates and load up the station wagon to head out to Brady's Run Park in Beaver Falls, Pennsylvania. This particular January 1969 outing included my brothers Paul and David, my friend Genevieve Rowan, me and my younger sister Marie.
SUSAN DIETRICH · MONACA, PA

LI'L POOKIE'S CREW ABANDONS SHIP

My brothers Alan, David and Gary, along with a neighborhood friend, Ronald Spivey, tried out their new boat in the driveway. This photo was taken in 1967 in Redford Township, Michigan.
GARY WATTS SOUTHPORT, NC

KIDS LOVED DAD'S WINTER PHOTO SHOOTS

On snowy days in the late 1940s and early 1950s, I went skiing with my brothers. My dad was always looking for the perfect picture. Here Dad used the seat, handlebars and front frame of a bicycle to make me a "ski-mobile."
MARGE VAN HEUKLON · KAUKAUNA, WI

IS THIS RIGHT?
My sister, Betsy, had no idea how to put up this tent during our family's camping vacation to the Grand Tetons in 1958.
DAVID HOLT · NATHROP, CO

LUNCH BREAK
While my steak was grilling, I snapped this picture of my wife, Joyce, daughter Ann, 4, and son Steve, 6, while we were on a camping trip in Door County, Wisconsin, in August 1958.
BRUCE THOMPSON · WAUKESHA, WI

THE GREAT NORTHWEST
In 1957, we packed up our '55 Ford station wagon, and camped all the way from Michigan to our grandparents' home in Port Angeles, Washington, where we lined up for this picture. From left, it's me, Tim, Beth, Dan and Jean.
JERI MAHLER · DEARBORN, MI

Search for African American Family History

Enslaved ancestor's job offered possible clue to lineage.

George Washington Fagan, born on a Virginia plantation, was freed while working off the plantation owner's debt.

As the family historian, I found that my great-great-grandfather, George Washington Fagan, was born in 1819 in Buckingham County, Virginia. Several facts in my sources point to George's father being the plantation owner. First, George was taught to read and write. In addition, as a youngster, his primary duty was to keep the "master's big black boots clean and shiny." Then, as a young man, he acted as a foreman for the operation of the plantation. Last, he appeared in the 1870 census under the classification "mulatto."

George's owner was in debt to a plantation owner in Albemarle County, Virginia. Apparently, as part of an agreement, George and several other slaves were sent to that plantation to work off their owner's debt. Fortunately for them, the Civil War ended and the slaves were freed. Of his own free will, my great-great-grandfather stayed in Albemarle County, where the strong roots of our family tree were planted.

George's first marriage was to a woman referred to in my sources as "a Riffin girl." She died some time after their only child, Ardelia, was born in 1847. His second marriage, to Angeline Randolph, produced 10 children—an important and dynamic branch of our family tree.

Ardelia Fagan married Harry Armstead, who during "slavery times … was put up for sale four times," my sources said. Each time, Harry's master was not satisfied with the offers he received and, therefore, did not sell him. The 1880 census listed Harry as a farmhand; the 1900 census showed him owning his own farm "free and clear."

Harry and Ardelia had 10 children, including my grandmother, Bessie, who was born in 1890. She was able to get a third- or fourth-grade education and described to me how she wrote her lessons on a piece of slate.

Her husband, John Washington, born in 1887, could not read or write. I remember him marking an "X" on his paychecks so that my grandmother could cash them. I discovered John in the 1900 census, where he was listed as 13 and classified as a full-time farmhand.

Bessie and John had seven children, including my wonderful mother, Louise, born in 1923. I am the oldest of five children. Born in 1943, I am named after my great-grandfather, Harry Armstead, born 100 years earlier in 1843.

Although research indicates that some of our ancestors bore the yoke of slave experience, it also shows that they triumphed over this negative history with strength of character, religious belief and a firm commitment to self-development and survival of the family.

Our family tree has thrived because of its strong roots. Descendants of the enslaved boy who shined his master's boots have succeeded in such diverse professions as law, medicine, banking, history and research, real estate, music, the military, education and the ministry.

HARRY JAMES FORD · PITTSBURGH, PA

A typical manifest from a slave ship—this one showing six slaves, identified by their first names only. The vessel docked at New Orleans in 1832.

Escape from the Iron Curtain

Facing arrest, a young revolutionary fled his homeland.

W My father, Joseph Bota, was born in 1938 in Balatonfured, Hungary, which the Nazi army entered a few years later. After the war, the occupying Russians deemed his father, a local butcher, to be a capitalist and confiscated his property and businesses.

My father, then 18, his cousin Laszlo and friend Laci, along with many other students, demonstrated against the communist regime. On Oct. 23, 1956, the Soviet military intervened, killing many revolutionaries. Warned of coming arrests, and knowing the fate of prisoners, Dad and six others hired a truck driver to take them to the Austrian border. At the meeting point with the driver, Dad, Laszlo and Laci saw their friends being arrested. They hid, and then took a commuter train, finally making it to within a few hundred yards of the mined and electrified border. There they met hundreds of fellow citizens trying to cross. Hungarian guards drew their weapons, questioning them, but then wished them well and stood aside.

Crawling between railroad tracks, they crossed the border into Austria at 4 a.m. on Nov. 21. Near the end of the following May, Dad made it to the United States.

The Presbyterian Church arranged a sponsor, and eventually Dad and Laszlo landed in New Castle, Indiana. (Laci ultimately settled in Germany.) Dad never stopped loving his home country of Hungary, but he always reminds my brother and me how lucky we are to have grown up here.

KAROLINE BOTA · RIO RANCHO, NM

Laci, Joe and Laszlo in Salzburg, Austria, in 1957, after their escape.

Roger's grandparents Sarah and Ira, center, with four of their sons.

Observing Decoration Day

Yearly graveyard gatherings renewed family ties.

Decoration Day, which falls at the end of May, was a revered social event of the Appalachian people, even more so than Christmas. Generations of relatives gathered in cemeteries to remember loved ones.

I never knew Grandpa or Granny Guffey, Uncle Haywood or Uncle Charlie Lewis, but I learned much about my ancestors as we converged on churchyards around Wayne County, Kentucky. I heard not only about the war heroes but also about the everyday people, and in many cases, I learned how they met untimely ends.

I was to regard the deceased with veneration while I endeavored to add to our family legacy.

My siblings and I crafted flowers from crepe paper and wire, and planted them on ancestors' graves. We dressed in finery, sharing dinner on the ground under the oaks and hickories. I showed off my first clip-on necktie at Decoration Day.

The exodus of the mountain people for jobs in cities changed those rhythms, and now most communities no longer celebrate Decoration Day. I change the flowers on my parents' graves to reflect the seasons, but I never see anyone else in the cemetery.

Now that the day is on my mind, it's time to order crepe paper.

ROGER GUFFEY · LEXINGTON, KY

KITCHEN CONFIDENTIAL

The mostest for the hostess.

1954 »

New Flame

This *Ladies' Home Journal* ad challenges the steel-electric alliance by showing a sleek culinary space of polished wood and gas appliances—which produces a perfectly cooked turkey.

Look to GAS for the
smartest ranges you ever saw!

Only **Gas** gives
such matchless performance

STEP INTO MY
Take-it-easy Kitchen
...and you'll find a wonderful new world
of efficiency and charm!

REPUBLIC STEEL *Kitchens*

« 1954

Clean Convenience

Republic was one of dozens of steel producers that retooled for the home market in the postwar building boom. Its Berger division began making kitchen cabinets in 1946. Steel dominated the market until about the mid-1960s, when wood cabinetry became the norm.

« 1953

Mull it with Mullins

Mullins Manufacturing Corp. was a top seller of kitchens in the 1950s housing boom, expanding its Youngstown line as soon as WWII ended. Diana the Huntress in the Youngstown logo is based on a sculpture commissioned by W.H. Mullins and exhibited at Chicago's Columbia Exposition in 1893.

1949 »

Life of the Party

An ad full of personality from General Electric. This ran in *The Saturday Evening Post* and clearly mimics the magazine's Norman Rockwell-led artistic vibe from the period. It's a perfect rendering of the host's dilemma—how to get guests out of the kitchen.

A kitchen that's always in a party mood

You can put your confidence in—

GENERAL ELECTRIC

A Flair for Repair

Handyman kept the whole neighborhood
in good working order.

A cross the front of the sweatshirt I held up to show my husband, Don, was the phrase "Grandpa: The Man, The Myth, The Legend." "Will Dad wear this?" I asked. "Probably not," he said.

I knew Don was right. My dad, Bruce Musterman, was too humble to wear anything like that, despite his celebrated status in our family. He was the fix-it man, able to repair anything: the leaky hot water tank, the washing machine that refused to spin and the car air conditioner that blew hot air.

When I was 5, I got a Chatty Cathy doll, a 1960s miracle of toy technology. Everywhere I went, Cathy went, too, until she was no longer chatty. I was devastated. But I should have known that a dad who could repair refrigerators could figure out how to make Chatty Cathy talk again.

Dad saved my Brownie camera and my junior scientist microscope. He fixed my brother's cap pistols and little toy cars with windup motors. We got frequent phone calls from the neighbors requesting his expertise. Was that engine idling too fast? Did someone's dishwasher have a leak? Was the church having plumbing problems? Call Bruce!

When he occasionally ran out of things to overhaul, he built something new: a cabinet, a garage, a back porch with stairs.

As a teen, I looked up to my dad less and less. His limitless ability to fix things didn't work for my problems with friends, or help my angst over homework or career choices. My grumpiness didn't seem to bother Dad. When my car broke down and I called him for help, he just fixed it.

When I married Don, he wasn't a handyman. But over the years, my dad helped him replace the roof on our home and repair our major household appliances.

With Dad as a master teacher, I figured my husband would inherit Dad's DIY crown.

To everyone's surprise, our youngest daughter, Teresa, is the one who's taken on that role, and she now wears the tool belt in the family. That girl can fix anything.

My dad is now in his 90s and can no longer lift things or handle heavy tools. Teresa encourages him to "supervise" when she is doing a repair, and we remind him she inherited her handiness from him.

DIANNA GRAVEMAN · PALM HARBOR, FL

Bruce's knack for fixing stuff made him a legend. Here he is in a rare idle moment in '57.

The Hessons posed for a photo after Jim came home from WWII. "You can see the joy and relief and hope in our eyes," Jana writes.

Silver Token of Love and Thanks

Returning soldier's gift embraced his peacetime dream.

My father, Jim Hesson, was drafted into the Army in 1943 during World War II. Mom, Anna, was pregnant with me when Dad was deployed overseas. She gave up their cozy apartment in Baltimore, Maryland, and moved in with my grandparents to await my birth. Mom worked at American Can Co. as the sole breadwinner for us. Though young, I remember the highlight of my day was waiting for her to walk down our alley each night from her streetcar stop.

I was 3 when Daddy returned safely, with bright hopes of creating a good life for his family. On Mother's Day that year, he gave Mom a lovely silver locket with her initial in filigree on the front and engraved on the back with "Love Jana Daddy 1946." Inside were photos of me in my bonnet and on Daddy's shoulders. It was his way of expressing his love and gratitude for Mom's devotion while he was away.

A brother and sister arrived within the next three years. Daddy became a gifted church organist, but died early at 65. Thankfully, I have his knapsack, dog tags and Good Conduct Medal as reminders of his valor. On my 50th birthday, Mom gave me the locket in a velvet-lined, heart-shaped box as we exchanged tearful hugs. Mom is still with us, and those war years are still vividly with her. My lovely locket will always be a precious memento of those challenging but happy days.

JANA PEACH · GIBSONVILLE, NC

FOCUS ON: STIEFF

Jana's locket photos are glued in, hiding identifying marks, but she is fairly certain it was made by Stieff Co., a venerable smith of silver and pewter in Baltimore since the 1890s. Better known for flatware, Stieff sold jewelry and other non-tableware in its retail stores. Stieff jewelry is on online auction sites, but lockets like Jana's can be hard to find. Recent jewelry prices range from about $10 to $300 or more, depending on the item's style and age.

Old Tom and young Kenny stand nose to nose in the Iowa barnyard in 1923.

Agricultural Revolutions

Tom's horsepower came with friendly nudges.

When I was 1½, I went to live on Uncle Bill and Aunt Astrid's farm in northwestern Iowa. The farm work was done by horses—tractors were just a dream back in the early 1920s—and I soon bonded with Tom.

Tom had celebrity status on the farm: He pulled the bobsled in wintertime, and we rode him to round up the milk cows. His big job was being the circle horse. During the weekslong corn harvest, Tom powered the elevator that carried corn to the top of the storage bin.

When Tom was harnessed to the unit, Bill moved the load of corn into place and set Tom in motion with a "giddyup." When Tom's slow circles got even slower, Bill, stationed in the wagon near the hopper, would toss an ear of corn at Tom's rump to get him to pick up the pace.

Bill's deadly accurate throws always reminded me that former Cleveland Indians pitcher and baseball Hall of Famer Bob Feller was a farm boy, too. I thought Bill should have tried out for the Major Leagues.

Tom had certain privileges. In hot weather, he was allowed to back out of the open barn door and get himself a drink at the water tank. If I was in the yard, he'd come over to give me a friendly rub with his nose. I frequently went past his stall and felt his nose on my back.

After Tom died, no horse replaced him.

We had a Chevy truck we drove to round up the cows, and a John Deere tractor powered the corn elevator. Over time, we found the costs worked out to be about the same: Tom's oats were 8 cents a bushel and the gas the Chevy burned was 15 cents a gallon.

I headed off to college in 1938. When I came home I walked past my old friend Tom's empty stall, expecting to feel him tip my hat or rub his nose on my back.

KENNETH ARMSTRONG · STORM LAKE, IA

Twins Give Dad a New Job

Elmer was expert at washing diapers.

When Elmer and I realized I was pregnant, I went to visit a doctor in Inglewood, California. We were living in Santa Monica at the time. Everything was fine at that first visit, but the doctor did ask me if there were twins in my family. I told him no, and he told me not to worry about it. We didn't worry about it, and I didn't ever see that doctor again.

Elmer's cousin Harold Alexander was in medical school in Los Angeles. He insisted that I get under the care of his favorite practicing instructor, Dr. Reynolds. It was a long way for us to drive, so the doctor only saw me once a month—he said I was doing so well that I didn't need to come more often. I would pick up Elmer at Douglas Aircraft Co., where he worked as a tool and die maker, and he would shave and change his clothes on the lengthy ride to the doctor's office.

We didn't have a phone in 1940—there was a waiting list to get one at that time. Late on July 2, we decided I should go to the hospital. By the time we were driving down Olympic Boulevard in Santa Monica, it was 1 a.m. There was not much traffic, so Elmer just slowed down at the red signals. Soon here came a cop who pulled us over for not coming to complete stops. He took one look at me and let us go.

Larry arrived at 8:59 a.m. July 3 and Lloyd, two minutes later. Someone woke up dear Elmer, who was asleep in the waiting area—fathers weren't allowed in the delivery room then—and told him I'd had twins. It was a surprise to everyone.

I didn't know how I was going to manage one, let alone two, but Elmer was a rock.

He washed diapers for one year—that was before disposables became common, of course.

I loved California and thought we'd stay there forever, but just before the boys turned 6, we moved to southern Oregon because we wanted to raise our sons in a less-populated area. We will always be thankful we have such wonderful sons.

RUBY HELEN SMITH · PHOENIX, OR

Larry and Lloyd were about 3 in this picture. Their mother, Ruby, wrote this story for them in 2001. She died in 2008 at age 91.

Someone woke up dear Elmer...and told him I'd had twins. It was a surprise to everyone.

Harvey and Audrey at a signing for their book about Tandy the elf.

A Home for Book Lovers

Authors' legacy is sharing the power of a story.

A mong the pages of my photo album are many containing snapshots of my parents, Harvey and Audrey Hirsch, smiling and full of life. Thankfully, the sadness of missing them is quickly replaced with pride that the works of art they created together live on.

Dad told me and my three sisters stories of growing up in the 1930s with a single mom who was too poor to buy him a book. He desperately wanted to read, and his longing for books explained why our childhood home was filled with so many of them.

After their marriage in 1955, my parents lived in Arizona, where Dad taught English at Arizona State University, then called Arizona State College. Mom, with my big sister Cheri in tow, managed the trailer park where they lived.

One hot afternoon, as she and Cheri sat under a tree to cool off, Mom became inspired to write a children's story about an elf named Tandy who was trying to find a home before winter. With the help of all the woodland characters, Tandy was able to do just that.

Dad loved the story, and my parents worked on it together. I was 8 when Dad got a new job and we moved to Michigan. Seeing snow for the first time, I felt a bit like Tandy the elf.

In 1971, children's publishing house Platt & Munk Co. published their book *A Home for Tandy*, illustrated by twins Tim and Greg Hildebrandt. Those artists went on to illustrate the *Star Wars* movie posters.

I was 12 when I watched my parents smile at patrons of a local bookstore during their first book signing. They wrote many more books for children, and I continue their legacy by sharing my love of reading with others. Now in my 60s, I write and illustrate children's books, and I volunteer as a reading mentor. There is no greater gift than seeing a child's self-confidence grow when they learn to enjoy the power of words.

REBECCA SPOHN · AUBURN, MI

A Perfectly Imperfect Picture

At the Detroit Zoo in 1963, my family went from posed to
chaos as the shutter clicked. I'm on the bottom left.

TIM TANGO · WESTHAMPTON BEACH, NY

CHAPTER 3

TRUE LOVE

From wartime romances to high school sweethearts, dive into tales of meant-to-be love that'll warm your heart.

Young Hearts

Virginia Parnham, my mother-in-law, was a high school student in
Des Moines and Bob Ferguson attended Drake University when they
eloped in 1940. They kept it a secret and went back to their homes.

JANE FERGUSON · ALTOONA, IA

The Salzmans with children Elaine, Romy, Carolyn, Jim and Rog in 1953.

Learning from the Best

Mom and Dad show how to share a rich life together.

D ad, Tony Salzman, was born in the small community of Cassel, Wisconsin, near Wausau, in 1913. He had a great sense of humor: He always told us kids that he was born in a castle. Our mom, Edna Hanke, was born in Rib Falls, another small town about 4½ miles from Cassel, in 1914. They were married just shy of 50 years. Dad worked at what became 3M Co. for five decades. But his wife and family were always the most important part of his life.

He made me feel that I was his favorite child, but I think all five of his kids felt the same way. He and Mom loved when the family got together.

Mom and Dad had a special relationship that was more romantic than any of us realized. When I was packing up Mom's possessions a few years ago, I found dozens of valentines that Dad sent her over the years.

My parents enjoyed traveling, especially with the camper that was Dad's pride and joy. They taught us kids to appreciate all living things, from woolly bear caterpillars to large wild animals. In summer, they liked to drive to a special place after dark, where they would roll down the windows and listen to the frogs.

Mom and Dad had this nut or gall about the size of a walnut that they must have found on one of

*In summer, they liked to drive to a
special place after dark, roll down the windows
and listen to the frogs.*

their many walks. We called it the knot. For years,
they gave it to each other as a gift. Dad would wrap
it up with a big bow and set it aside for Mom to
open, and she would make a big fuss as she did.
The next Christmas, Easter or Father's Day, or on
his birthday, the knot would appear all wrapped for
Dad to open. They kept up this exchange for most
of their marriage.

Every time the knot was being presented again,
Mom and Dad glanced at each other and smiled.
We kids would roll our eyes at them. Oh, there
they go again!

I'll never forget that look they used to give each
other. I'm sure they didn't realize it at the time, but
they were showing us that it made no difference
how much a gift cost or how big it was—what
mattered was the joy of giving and receiving.

Mom and Dad showed us what real love looks
like, and that it should be treasured.

I found their love knot packed away with Mom's
things. Today, I have it tucked close with my
favorite mementos.

ELAINE LANG · KRONENWETTER, WI

Tony and Edna enjoyed a rare friendship and love through
almost 50 years of marriage. Top, they hold hands in front of
nephew Gerald Hanke in 1934; Bottom, dancing in the 1960s.

Plan to Impress Goes Awry

She acted on friendship, but the guy turned down the roll.

———

W hen I was a sophomore in high school, one of my hobbies was baking. I started making cookies and cakes, and went on to learn to make yeast breads.

In 1967, at the county fair in Chelan, Washington, I competed in a three-hour breadmaking contest. The event was live, and fairgoers watched me demonstrate the process. One woman watched my demonstration and when I finished, told me what a great job I did.

I felt good about the demonstration, too, and decided to share some of the blue-ribbon dinner rolls with a boy that I liked. I found him in the rabbit barn, but when I offered the rolls to him, he said, "No, thank you." I gave the bread to other friends and walked back to the kitchen to clean up.

The woman who watched my demonstration noticed my dejection. I explained that my friend, Randy, whom I had wanted to impress, turned down my offer of rolls. She said, "Don't worry, he's spoiled because he gets homemade bread all the time."

When I saw Randy later, I told him about that encouraging woman. Randy knew who I meant: "She's my mom." She had known all along who I was trying to impress!

That lovely woman has been my mother-in-law for 45 years. And I still make the same recipe when I want to make points with someone.

SHELIA OGLE · WENATCHEE, WA

Shelia enjoyed home economics projects: She sewed the dress that she wore to junior prom, left, and to a formal dance, above.

ENROLLING FOR LIFE

AS I FILLED OUT MY SCHEDULE at the University of Missouri, where I was studying journalism under the GI Bill, I felt a tap on my shoulder. I turned to see a pretty blonde named Joy. She asked for help with some paperwork, and I asked her out to lunch.

A month into the semester, we went to visit Joy's folks in Kansas City. I was from New Jersey, and naturally I was a bit nervous to meet them. As it turned out, rightly so. Her mother invited me into her sewing room to have what she called a little chat. Did I attend church? Which one? Did I smoke, drink or gamble? What had my life in the Navy been like? What were my grades?

After an hour of this, Joy's mother smiled and said, "I'm going to fix us a nice dinner. Welcome to the family."

A year later I proposed to Joy over the phone and, after what seemed to me a long time, she said yes. We got married in a small ceremony, took a Greyhound to St. Louis for a weekend honeymoon and then went back to finish the semester. I became a professor of English literature and Joy taught art at a junior high school. People loved Joy, and they tolerated me because they liked her so much. We were together for 72 years: Little did I know what I was getting into that day I sat down to enroll.

MICHAEL TIMKO · PLEASANTON, CA

YOUNG LOVE

DAILY VALENTINES

Shortly after my parents married, my dad, James, was drafted. He and my mom, Shirley, wrote longing, passionate letters every day for the two years he was in the Army. A sweet one from Dad in May 1955 says, "I got to bed at 11:35 and proceeded to dream of you."

MARK HERSHBERGER
AUDUBON, NJ

"TO MY DARLING ELLEN"

When my parents celebrated their 63rd anniversary, my dad, Bruce, re-read the poem he wrote to propose to my mom.

KRIS HOBSON · DALLAS, TX

THE BEST ICEBREAKER

As a fifth grade sports fan who followed Cleveland's teams, I knew little about hockey. But I was impressed when my sister Connie, a hockey cheerleader at Bowling Green State University in 1969, started dating one of the team's stars, Canadian Peter Badour. They're still married.

PATRICK CASSEDAY · CHARDON, OH

ROOM FOR THE CHAPERONE

Hazel Fredrick, my mother, rode to high school in a horse and buggy, so a date in George Schmaling's auto—with a rumble seat!—was pretty exciting in 1925. They married in 1927 in Janesville, Wisconsin.

JOAN JOHNSTON · LAKEMOOR, IL

Jerry and Helga on their wedding day in Hamburg, Germany, 1965.

Pyramid Scheme

Before he could marry, he had to fulfill globe-trotting quest.

While a high school student in Port Townsend, Washington, I adopted the notion that I couldn't get serious with anyone I dated until I saw the Great Pyramids of Egypt. I'd never been on an airplane and didn't have specific travel plans in mind, but I wanted to see the world before settling down. I continued to have this goal while attending the University of Washington as well as the first three years that I was enlisted in the Army.

I was stationed in Mainz, Germany, when I met and started dating Helga Kook in 1964. It soon became obvious that my vague guideline regarding world travel was going to be a problem. I either had to take action on my goals or abandon them, so I followed my longtime dream.

My active service was up on April 1, 1965, and on April 2, I flew to Cairo, Egypt, where I took a taxi out to the Great Pyramids in the Giza plain. Climbing to the top of the Cheops pyramid was permitted. I was in good shape, so I started up.

Soon an attendant stopped me and informed me that I needed to hire an official guide for the climb. I bought a permit and was assigned a frail old gentleman, who smiled as he displayed his official armband.

We started up one corner, climbing over the large blocks at a fast clip. When I'd made my way halfway up, I stopped to let him catch up, but I turned to find him only a few feet behind me and hardly winded. We were the only two on the pyramid that morning and we continued to the top, where the view was astounding. The top was flat, as the blocks at the pinnacle had been pilfered in some past century.

I asked the guide to take a picture of me with my Minox camera, proof I was at the Great Pyramids. Now, my goal was met. I was eligible for marriage.

After seeing the pyramids, I returned to my home state of Washington and got a civilian job. Helga was still in Germany, living with her parents in Hamburg. A few months later, we got engaged over the phone. Immigration laws prevented her from staying in the U.S. if we married here, so I flew back to Germany and we were married in 1965.

Helga became a U.S. citizen—we have children and now grandchildren, and we've been married 55 years. We have traveled extensively throughout the world, and we hope to do more.

JERRY HILSON · EVERETT, WA

Asking for a Friend

This pen pal request took a turn.

Pen pals were popular when I was a student nurse in the 1960s. My friend Carol was writing to one of her brother's buddies in the Navy, Eric, who was stationed at Guantanamo Bay, Cuba, and I asked her whether he had a friend who also would like a pen pal.

A few weeks later I got a letter from Eric. He requested a photo, but since he was still writing to Carol, I let him know that he was two-timing my friend. He replied that he was trying to learn more so he could find a good pen pal for me. I fell for that, and sent a photo. Soon Eric stopped writing letters to my friend.

When he sent me an awful-smelling letter filled with rubber caps from beer bottles, I wasn't sure what to think. But after he apologized and sent me a charm bracelet with a more appropriate

cap—a nurse's cap—I wrote to thank him. Now we had a strange camaraderie. We were both away from home—he from Michigan and I from Illinois—and were happy to be getting mail.

After many months and many more letters, Eric visited me at school in Iowa. On another leave, we flew to meet his parents in Michigan. It was my first flight, and like everyone did in those days, I dressed up for the trip. Eric even bought me a corsage.

On his next leave, in May 1965, we got married. I graduated from nursing school and he was assigned to Newport Naval Station, Rhode Island. At last, we were husband and wife in our own home.

Our letter writing continued after we were married, as he was often out to sea.

JEANETTE GRONDA · GROSSE ILE, MI

Student nurse Jeanette with her young Navy man Eric in 1965.

For Richer or for Poorer

Loving partnership was truly lifelong.

Theresa Burnham and Earl Frederick Skillings, my parents, were both born in the town of Pine Point, Maine, in 1924. Mom had three siblings, and Dad was one of nine. Their families lived near each other, and from the time they were in a playpen, the two were always spending time together.

When they were teenagers, they liked each other, but Mom was a tomboy and wanted nothing to do with romance. She graduated from Scarborough High School in 1944 and went to work first at the South Portland shipyard; then she worked at the New England Telephone and Telegraph Co. as a telephone operator. Like others in his family, Dad dropped out of school at 16 to help support his family, working as a painter and a lobsterman.

In 1943, Dad joined the Navy, serving on various aircraft carriers during World War II. He wrote to Mom, calling her his "cupcake" in the letters she saved. After Dad's honorable discharge in 1946, he asked Mom to marry him.

Although both of the families were poor, Mom came from a background of education, and Dad's family thought she was way out of his league. Their families told them the marriage wouldn't work out, but Dad and Mom didn't listen, and they got married in August 1947.

For several years, they lived with my grandparents. In 1958, my parents, along with their six children, got their own home in Scarborough. Dad continued lobstering before working as a truck driver, and Mom was a homemaker.

In 1974, when their 10th child turned 6, Dad retired from trucking and fulfilled their lifelong dream by buying a 150-acre farm in Frankfort. They learned about farming as they lived it, raising livestock, growing vegetables and tapping maple trees for syrup. They cut wood for heating and recycled everything they could.

My parents farmed for 31 years and were happily married for 59. Although they were poor, they raised us in a loving home, and they kept us from ever feeling like we were underprivileged.

And now I carry on the tradition of love and pride in family that they taught me.

RUBY SKILLINGS · AUGUSTA, ME

Theresa and Fred were playmates, and then they were sweethearts.

Robert married Marlene in 1958. His friend Larry, next to him, was the best man.

Marine Gives an Order

Friendly WAVE follows through.

My friend Larry Witt and I were Marines stationed at Naval Air Station North Island in Coronado, California, in 1957. The base served as home to several military units, including the Women Accepted for Volunteer Emergency Service. Marine barracks were responsible for perimeter security at the base, including patrolling the gates.

One day as I was standing duty at the main gate, a car with several WAVES came through. They were headed for town, and I jokingly asked the WAVES to bring me a cup of coffee when they returned to base.

I was still there when they came back, and to my great surprise, Petty Officer 3rd Class Marlene A. Westbrook handed me a cup of coffee. A few days later, Marlene and I ran into each other again, and this time we struck up a conversation.

We had no money for anything, but we fell in love anyway. I sold my 1932 Ford 3-Window Coupe hot rod for $200 to buy wedding rings, and our families gave us a church wedding in Denver. Larry was my best man.

The car would've been worth tens of thousands today, but I wouldn't trade it for the excellent deal we got. We're so proud of our three daughters— a mayor, an educator and a recently retired U.S. Navy chief—and we recently celebrated our 62nd anniversary, too.

My only regret is that I've lost track of Larry. I would love some help to reconnect with him.

ROBERT BRINKMAN · DENVER, CO

PUCKER UP!

Lips made perfect for kisses.

1948 »

Spare No Expense
Revlon was the undisputed leader in lipstick and nail polish in the postwar years, which gave it the confidence to spend big on advertising. Full-color photo print ads like this *Life* spot were pricey, and therefore rare, in the 1940s.

Twin *miracles* of matchless *splendour!*

REVLON'S *new Lastron* nail enamel and *All-Plus* lipstick

With the steadying plume brush, application is oh, so easy with either left or right hand!

Up! Up! Up! The soaring lucite plume on the magnificent Lastron bottle symbolizes its *infinite* perfection. For Revlon's new miracle Lastron nail enamel introduces the *charmed* life in wear . . . the *easy* life in application! It dries in split seconds. Ends smearing worries.
Matching it in fashion-brilliant genius color, is Revlon's new All-Plus lipstick! Just what the name implies . . . in its rich, silken texture, easy stroke-on, *prolonged* lip beauty!

For the *smartest* matching lips and fingertips in all the world!

« 1954

Temporary Wave
Gillette Co. bought the thriving Toni Permanent Wave Co. in 1948 in the midst of a diversification kick. Over the next few years, it introduced more Toni-branded products, but most of them failed. Viv appeared in 1954 and lasted only a few months, despite an exciting ad campaign featuring vibrant visuals like this one.

she's got **Viv**
(you can have it, too!)

new viv lipstick by *Toni* $1.10

It's not so much beauty as it is personal vibrancy and sparkle, and all those indefinable qualities that make everyone instantly aware of her.
For now there's a new lipstick that brings out all the vividness and sparkle of the real you with exciting colors that make you look and feel vividly alive. It's the new VIV lipstick by Toni. VIV's new *High-Chroma Formula* gives you the most vivid colors any woman has ever worn. Choose from six bright shades, each as sparkling as the vivid Coral you see here. Try VIV, that vivid new lipstick by Toni.

Comfortable, long-lasting and very, very vivid.

1946   **Brand Royalty**

Louis Philippe was a French-born businessman whose New York cosmetics company devised an indelible lipstick, which sold under various labels, including Angelus and Incarnat. That his own name was similar to a former French king's—Louis-Philippe —no doubt helped his brand. Philippe sold his company in 1933 to American Home Products, which continued to market the cosmetics under the decidedly sexier Louis Philippe name.

Striking it Rich

Miner helps young mother stuck in a hole.

My mother, Bernice, was living in the mining town of Butte, Montana, with her two children. She'd survived the Great Depression and the turmoil of World War II, but had been put in a new and difficult position when her husband, an alcoholic and a gambler, left for California. He supposedly went to build a new life for them, but a few months later, she received a goodbye note from him, along with a set of divorce papers.

Her ex-sister-in-law helped her find a small apartment and even paid the first month's rent. But Bernice was unable to find employment, and was facing eviction. With no idea from where the next meal would come, she considered one last possibility. Butte's economy relied on the mining industry, and she reasoned that the miners union might have funds available for women in need. Taking the children, she walked 2 miles to the miners union hall.

The receptionist told her she was not eligible to receive assistance from the union since she wasn't the wife of a miner. As my mother pleaded her case, she could see over the top of the office dividers a man with wavy brown hair. The man, union president Bill Mason, was listening to her story and deciding whether to intervene.

Bill and his family emigrated from Croatia when he was 10. Two years later, his father abandoned his wife and two children, and Bill dropped out of school and became a miner to support the family. Starting in the position of union steward, he worked his way up to president.

That day, Bill invited Bernice and her kids for lunch, and then he offered to take them out for dinner after work. It was the beginning of their courtship.

They married in 1947; I was born in 1948, and four years later, they purchased a new home in a subdivision near Butte. Dad often gave Mom a single rose as a reminder of his love, and he sometimes danced with her at the sink while she washed the dishes.

Dad died in an auto accident when I was 14. Even though I was young, I know my parents were deeply in love.

WILLIAM V. MASON · COLUMBUS, OH

Bernice was in trying circumstances when Bill overheard her story.

Doug fell for the barefoot blond girl in pedal pushers. He and Jan were married shortly after this was taken in 1965.

Drenched with Meaning

Deluge of letters meant the same thing.

Janice Cauthen was born in Haleyville, Alabama, eight days after me. Her family moved to Pannes Avenue in the eastern part of Compton, California, in 1959, and our family moved there a year later.

Our house was four doors away from theirs. One beautiful day, my mother had me trimming and watering our hedges. Three girls came down the sidewalk—I noticed Jan, a tall, skinny blonde in a yellow T-shirt and turquoise pedal pushers. She was barefoot. As they passed, I adjusted the nozzle of the hose, tested the range and sprayed them. They screamed and ran. As Jan went past, our eyes locked, and then with the stride of a gazelle, she left the others behind. It wasn't exactly love at first sight, but it was a spark.

Over the next two years of junior high, then high school, Jan and I became friends, occasionally dating. In the summer of 1964, the Cauthen family traveled back to Alabama and Jan asked me to take care of their dog. The day she left, I thought it would make her laugh to find a letter waiting when she got to her grandmother's house. I wrote her a letter that day, and the next. One day, I wrote two letters. By the time the family got to Alabama, everyone was talking about the girl who had a mailbox full of letters waiting for her.

The process of writing every day concentrated and defined my feelings toward her, and I began to relate to the phrase "Absence makes the heart grow fonder." Any doubts about my feelings vanished when I saw their family car back in the driveway one morning. I dropped everything and rushed to her door. Although they'd gotten in late, and Jan was tired, she greeted me warmly. Her kiss sealed the deal.

We married a year after high school; within a year, I was drafted, and one year after that, I was on my way to Vietnam.

We've been married 54 years, working side by side for most of them. We enjoyed raising our two sons—being their father is the great honor of my life. Looking back, maybe it was love at first sight.

DOUG DWYER · FALLBROOK, CA

The couple married just four weeks after meeting.

Make Hay While the Sun Shines

Furlough on the farm was life-changing.

———

Uncle Joe and Aunt Florence's hay crop on their farm in Lamoille, Nevada, was ready to harvest in 1954. Stationed at McChord Air Force Base in Tacoma, I took furlough to help.

In late July, I was mowing hay when Florence's sister—my aunt Ruby Catherine, called RC—and her husband, Jim, arrived from Mukilteo, Washington, for a visit. With them was a good-looking young woman I'd never met.

They introduced me to Evelyn, their children's babysitter. Evelyn had come with them because they didn't want to lose her to another family. In hindsight, they should not have brought her along if they wanted to keep her.

After dinner, my cousin Helen and I planned to go to a drive-in movie, and we invited Evelyn. Soon Evelyn and I were taking evening drives and talking about all kinds of things, including —finally—getting married when we got back to Washington, which was soon. My furlough would end in a few days.

Before I left on my furlough, I had plans to return to college. But when I got back to McChord, I reenlisted for six years, a move that provided us with a regular paycheck, as well as a $1,000 bonus.

Evelyn's dad suggested we put off our marriage long enough to plan a church wedding. He'd been buying wedding presents for relatives and friends for a long time, he said, and it was about time he got some in return. We agreed that this was a good idea.

We gave it two weeks.

In that time, Evelyn and her mother sent out invitations, bought a wedding dress and made all arrangements. I don't know how they did it. At our wedding on Aug. 28, 1954, we had more than 100 guests, and got a carload of gifts.

I rented a house near McChord, and as a wedding present, I gave Evelyn a fishing rod and a reel.

RAY ARNHOLD · TACOMA, WA

Longtime Love

Jean and I married on May 7, 1960, and began our life together for the
next 54 years, five months and 16 days. She was my best gal.

RICHARD OBROSKY · BROKEN ARROW, OK

CHAPTER 4

FADS, FASHION, FUN

From Goldfish to Chanel suits and everything in-between, there was plenty to admire about popular culture and style back in the day.

Pint-Size Fashion

My sisters Diane and Dawn (in wagon) and I bundle up to play
one cool day in Huntingdon Valley, Pennsylvania, in 1963.

DOREEN KIRBAN FRICK · ORD, NE

This vacation picture of John, mom Madeline and Wynne is from the period when they liked going to Rhodes.

Rhodes Trip

Six wonderful floors beckoned the family to the city.

in the 1940s, we took the bus downtown from the suburbs outside Tacoma, Washington, to do some shopping. My mother, Madeline, let my brother and me roam in our favorite sections of Rhodes Brothers Department Store, but she took us through some pretty uninteresting parts of the store first.

The men's department was on the first floor. There, everything seemed to be only in white—handkerchiefs, shirts, boxer shorts. The ties came

in sensible colors. Women's clothing, on another floor, was more elaborate, but woe to the shopper who was tall or petite—no special sizes.

Sequestered in the back corner of the first floor was the least exciting section of them all—the sewing notions.

There my mother bought scissors, assorted buttons, tape measures and pins. This was also where she discreetly shopped for dress shields to sew into the underarms of her outfits. In cahoots with notions was the fabric department, which, for

I tried on Oxfords and slid my feet into the machine, looking down through the window at my murky green skeleton feet.

some reason, was on a different floor. Once past these trials, I could wander in the music and book sections, which I loved.

The white-gloved elevator operator moved us from floor to floor by turning a big golden wheel. She'd trill, "Up car, gooooing up," sometimes overshooting a floor before getting us back on track. She knew where everything was located in the store and dutifully recited the contents of each floor.

Rhodes' music department had record albums for $1. Sheet music was also available, and there was even a clerk willing to pound out the melody on an old upright piano. In the book department, I could buy a Nancy Drew or Hardy Boys mystery for 75 cents.

Most fascinating of all was the children's footwear department, which had an X-ray machine.

I tried on Oxfords—always Oxfords—and slid my feet into the machine, looking down through the window at my murky green skeleton feet. This was the scientific way to determine if the shoes we might purchase had enough growing room.

When it was time to pay, my mother handed over her Rhodes charge card. The clerk placed everything in a cylinder and pushed a button. The cylinder whooshed away to the hidden depths where such things were taken care of. A few minutes later, the process was reversed and the cylinder returned, bringing the receipt.

"Hon," my dad would yell to my mother on the first of every month, "where's the Rhodes bill?" Our Rhodes card was the only charge card our family had, and Dad paid it off diligently.

Rhodes got a few modern touches over the years, some of which were met with excitement—others, with a little apprehension. In the 1950s, they added a revolving front door. We kids went around and around, until some adult came to show us the error of our ways. And when Rhodes finally ripped out its stairs and installed an escalator, there was a big to-do. We rode to the top on the moving stairs, hoping that our feet wouldn't disappear right into the mysterious mechanism.

No trip to Rhodes was complete without a visit to the soda fountain on the mezzanine, where they made the best-ever hot fudge sundaes.

Long gone, Rhodes is only a distant memory, but a happy one.

WYNNE CROMBIE · HUNTLEY, IL

BIG BOX CORNERS THE MARKET

American officials in the 1950s began to backpedal on domestic trade laws that looked out for mom and pops. Big companies were allowed to get volume discounts, ushering in the age of retail's mark-down giants: Walmart, Target, Kmart and Kohl's opened their first stores in 1962. Shoppers accepted a lower level of service than they got at the department stores that reigned on Main Street, since the goods were similar and the prices were lower.

Walton's 5&10 opened in 1950 in Bentonville, Arkansas. It inspired owner Sam Walton to launch a discount chain, with the first store in neighboring Rogers in 1962.

....

Wide aisles, fast checkout and parking for 1,200 cars: The Dayton Co. planned for a new way to shop at Target, its proposed discount store in Roseville, outside of Minneapolis.

....

The S.S. Kresge Co. operated five-and-dimes and dollar stores. In 1962, the company opened its first discount department store—Kmart—in Garden City, Michigan. By the end of that year, they'd opened 17 more.

....

Maxwell Kohl was a grocer when he opened his first department store in Brookfield, Wisconsin. Positioned between premium department stores and five-and-dimes, Kohl's found a niche that was just right.

NATALIE WYSONG

Good as Gold

Sibling relationship finds a new gear.

My brother Joey and I shared a bike—an English racer—and we each got to use it for a week at time in 1971, when I was 16.

It was his week to have the bike, but I needed to get to the Gimbel Brothers department store in Upper Darby, Pennsylvania. I had just pierced my ears, and I wanted to buy my first pair of grown-up earrings. But when I asked Joey if I could take the bike, he said "Nope," and pedaled away.

Since Joey was being a bum, I had to walk the 4 miles because I didn't want to pay for the bus ride. I'd saved exactly what I needed for the 24K gold earrings, which were advertised for $15.24.

At the store, the clerk brought out the velvet box with the coveted jewelry. But when she rang up the purchase, it was a little more than I had. There had to be a mistake! The saleswoman gave me an understanding smile, and said, "Honey, that price did not include the tax."

My face reddened with shame as I closed the box and whispered that I wasn't able to afford the earrings. I couldn't even look the woman in the face as I thanked her, and then I left.

I had very few options for earning extra money, but I thought maybe I could do some chores in the neighborhood for some people who would give me money instead of paying me with a sandwich. Looking along the railroad tracks for soda bottles that I could return for the deposit was also worth a shot.

Then, surprisingly, the saleswoman tapped my shoulder. Impressed that I'd come to Gimbels just to buy the earrings, her manager had given the OK for me to buy them at a slight discount.

Getting around the neighborhood meant Joey and Kathleen had to share a bike.

I floated out of the store with my treasure in a bag. There on the curb sat my brother with the bicycle. Certain that I was up to something, he'd followed me.

This might have been the only time I wasn't mad at Joey for spying on me. He offered me a ride home on the handlebars, and he even complimented my earrings.

KATHLEEN DOLL CRISTOFARO
ALDAN, PA

Mobo remains a favorite in the D'Ammora family. Devin, Antoinette's granddaughter, has a go in 2008.

Bucking the Trend

Vintage Mobo riding horse still showing its mettle after more than 70 years.

Somewhere around 1949, at the age of 4 or 5, my husband, Joe, received an interesting —and enduring—gift from his paternal Grandpa Andre: a metal riding horse Joe named Mobo. That was the maker's name stamped on the stirrups, and Joe kept it. Mobo riding horses inch along, slowly, when the child presses down on the stirrups. It's hard work, but at least it's a fairly safe ride.

We still have Mobo. We like to say in our family that everyone gets to own Mobo, but for a short time. All small children get to enjoy the ride and wonder over this antique and rather noisy mode of transportation. After all, Mobo is aged, so he's cranky.

Joe loved Mobo, but his lasting memory of the toy is how his brother Vic, who was seven years younger, used to turn Mobo upside down and fiddle with the stirrups, wheels and gears, waking up Joe every morning with the racket. The boys shared a bedroom in a Bronx apartment, so there was nowhere for Joe to escape the noise.

Mobo entertained our daughters, especially our youngest, Maria, and then Vic's children. He was back with Maria for her children for a while, and now he's with Vic's children, who each have kids of their own. Mobo will outlive us all. We've never touched up or replaced his paint—to preserve his original look. He ages naturally.

ANTOINETTE D'AMMORA · BETHPAGE, NY

FOCUS ON: MOBO BRONCO

The Mobo Bronco ride-on horse like the one owned by the D'Ammoras was a popular toy made by the U.K.'s D. Sebel & Co. beginning in 1947. Sebel toys were in high demand in America, and in 1948 the company set up a subsidiary in New York. Mobo Toys ceased production in 1972. Today, vintage Broncos can fetch high prices on online auction sites. One was listed at $1,300 recently. Most start around $250.

Goldfish were a little bit serious when they came on the scene in 1962—the sweet smiles came later.

Hooked on Goldfish

Little crackers crossed the ocean.

Admirers of Swiss ingenuity, nibble on this: In 1958, Oscar Kambly, a biscuit maker in Switzerland's Emmental region, invented a fish-shaped snack in honor of his wife, a Pisces.

Entrepreneur Margaret Rudkin, founder of Pepperidge Farm, tasted the little crackers while touring in Switzerland. A foodie who got into the bakery business when she developed a homemade bread for her son with food allergies, Rudkin sought out old-world recipes and premium products to add to the Pepperidge Farm line. She introduced Goldfish to the U.S. in 1962, where they've become a top-selling snack, munched on by everyone from the kindergarten snack brigade to the happy hour set.

NATALIE WYSONG

Dive into the Numbers
One fish, two fish...

1937

The year Margaret Rudkin founded Pepperidge Farm. Rudkin baked her first loaves in her Connecticut farmhouse kitchen, and then expanded into the family's garage. Rudkin lowered production during the war so she wouldn't have to compromise on the quality of the ingredients. By the time the company moved into a custom-designed plant in Norwalk after a decade in business, Pepperidge Farm was baking 40,000 loaves per hour.

3

The number of medals U.S. Allies awarded to Ralph Hauenstein, Nazi-code breaker and Goldfish cracker equipment manufacturer. Hauenstein wanted to help countries rebuild after WWII. Inspired by a German baker whom he saw creating fish-shaped crackers, Hauenstein developed equipment to mass-produce the little snacks. He shared the cracker-making equipment with the baker, and he also sold it to Pepperidge Farm for millions.

1.7 MILLION

The distance in miles Goldfish traveled in 1988 when the crew of the space shuttle Discovery took the crackers along for an out-of-this-world snack.

2

The number of items found on Julia Child's pre-meal Thanksgiving menu: Goldfish crackers and her own version of martinis.

$608.3 MILLION

Sales for Goldfish crackers in 2019. The "flavor blasted" varieties, such as Burstin' BBQ and Xtra Cheddar, were hot sellers at $175.6 million.

35

That's how many years it took before Goldfish cracked a smile. Next time you grab a handful, take a closer look. In every bag, only about 40% of the little guys are grinning.

$28 MILLION

The amount Rudkin got for Pepperidge Farm when she sold it to Campbell Soup Co. in 1960. Rudkin became Campbell's first female board member.

Margaret Rudkin's first baking efforts used her Irish grandmother's whole wheat bread recipe.

25

The price for a loaf of Pepperidge Farm bread, when the going rate was 10 cents. "Health bread," made with stone-ground wheat and local honey, it had an instant following.

DOZENS

Original, Cheddar, Graham, Xplosive Pizza—Goldfish come in lots of flavors, including limited and seasonal editions.

PASTIMES

» DAYS BY THE BAY

In 1946, we moved to Carman Bay on Lake Minnetonka in Minnesota. My brother Jack, sister Peg and I, and our seven siblings ran carefree, interrupted occasionally by the aroma of Mom's apple pies baking.
PAT SOLSTAD
WOODBURY, MN

❥ SCOOTER PROUD

For my 11th birthday, my parents, Herman and Mary Feldman, gave me this new scooter. The look on my face says it all!
RON FELDMAN
SAGINAW, MI

UNDER CONSTRUCTION

My brother Ben Haughawout, in front, joined in our cousins' engineering project at a family reunion in the 1950s. I really love that old car in the background.
BECKY BORES · MONROEVILLE, OH

BEFORE DUSK
My brothers and I (center front) and our friends head home from the park one afternoon in the early 1940s. We lived in Linnton, part of Portland, and our fathers worked at local sawmills. The pail at Johnny Ricks' feet probably is home-stove oil.
BERNARD VERBOUT · PORTLAND, OR

All Ears for Baby Elephant's Story

Librarian's large heart turns around childish mistake.

When I was 8, I stole a book from the Cobbs Creek Branch of the Free Library of Philadelphia. It was the story of Dumbo, a baby circus elephant whose huge ears allowed him to fly.

This was a special edition of the book—Dumbo's skin had a rough texture that enticed my small fingers. I re-borrowed the book several times until the children's librarian told me gently that other boys and girls wanted to read it, too, and that I could check it out only once more.

I strongly identified with Dumbo, the outcast, and was determined to keep the treasured book. At home, I scribbled out the branch name, ripped the pocket out of the book and tore up the date-due card. Then I hid the book in my room under my mattress. During spring cleaning, my mother turned my mattress and found the book. She marched me to the library and right up to the children's librarian.

The librarian was kind, and she suggested that I do chores in the library to work off my fine. I was mortified, and it was only her sensitive approach and my confidence in her forgiveness that gave me the courage to keep visiting that library.

Years later, I became a children's librarian and worked my entire 40-year career for the Free Library system. I'd forgotten the librarian's name, but as a consultant in the library's Office of Work with Children, I had access to files and I found her. She was still a librarian, a colleague in the office I worked in. It was gratifying to be able to thank her for the way she handled a tender situation and for her influence on my life.

LINDA FEIN · PHILADELPHIA, PA

A little understanding went a long way when Linda tried to keep a favorite library book.

Kathy shows off her bike—and a pair of Mary Janes—to her cousins in 1961.

The Shoes Make the Child

Wearing the right footwear was important.

——

Red or blue shoes, dress or play shoes? Barbara Manning, my mom, taught me that the choice mattered. Dress shoes were to be worn only for Mass and catechism—white at Easter and black at Christmastime.

My new scuff-free T-straps had teardrop-shaped eyelet holes and grosgrain ribbon trim. When I couldn't squeeze them on, even with a shoehorn, and the patent finish was creased and cracked from walking, it was time for another pair.

We got new ones when our dad, Jack, sent the Hereford cattle to market, and even at 6 I knew that wasn't often.

When I was 9, canvas tennis shoes were the rage. They were an improvement on the usual summer footwear: flip-flops, which made me trip and stub my toes. The shoe clerk at Sears measured my feet for the right size, and Mom helped me pick navy blue. "It'll hide the dirt better," she said.

In fifth grade I scored a pair of sassy red Mary Janes with cutouts on the uppers and a buckled strap. At bedtime the day I got them, I gave the shoes one last look before turning out my lamp. When I awoke during the night, I checked that they were safe.

Soon I wanted the pumps that all the other preteen girls had. These training shoes were slip-ons without straps to keep them on my feet. I walked—never ran—in those short, chunky heels until I didn't trip or fall down steps. Mom said there was one more snag to maturity: nylons.

KATHLEEN WEBER · LANARK, IL

Printing staff and customers in front of Librairie Evangelique.

Succumbing to Wanderlust

Bookkeeper invested a year in West Africa.

A student at Southern California College (now Vanguard University) from 1959 to 1962, I'd changed my major three times. I felt "schooled out" and was excited when I located a program that allowed me to travel in exchange for my bookkeeping skills.

I signed up for Youth with a Mission, and in October 1962, I said goodbye to my family at the airport in Casper, Wyoming, and I flew to West Africa to begin my year there.

As we descended into Ouagadougou, the capital of Haute Volta (now Burkina Faso), I could see that the downtown was filled with large modern buildings while the surrounding homes were straw huts. That first day, Mrs. Jones, the wife of the missionary I was to work for, took me to the outdoor market; as with everything I'd seen, I fell in love with it.

My bookkeeping job was working for a missionary, Harold Jones, at his Librairie Evangelique (Evangelical Bookstore).

Above: At the airport in Casper, Marian is flanked by brother Ken, 15, parents, Ople and Elmer, and sister Connie, 11. Left: After days of seasickness, Marian, third from left, finally met her table mates on the ship.

The bookstore had an attached print shop that employed several locals, and it was a major stopping place in the community. Next door was the Protestant church, where I played keyboard. The church was filled to capacity every Sunday.

It was a marvelous year.

I made many friends among the American and French missionaries, as well as my African co-workers, and learned to speak French well. My letters home were full of details of the bookstore and my life in West Africa.

In November 1963, my year was up, but I'd gone past the return date on my round-trip flight. I had to sail home on the SS *United States*. I was delighted!

When I awoke the first morning on the swaying ship, I was very sick. For three days, I went to the top deck, wrapped myself in blankets, and curled up on a cot at the center of the ship where there was less movement, returning to my room only at night. I'll never forget the kindness of the steward on that deck.

I finally recovered and met my table mates in the dining room for the first time. Two of them, brothers from Scandinavia, welcomed me like I was part of the family.

The *United States* docked in New York Harbor on Nov. 22, 1963. There I was greeted with the news that President John F. Kennedy had been assassinated in Dallas, Texas, that very afternoon. What a shock.

My family lived in Wyoming, so they couldn't meet me. But luckily an American friend I'd made in Ouagadougou was there to welcome me back.

MARIAN ROSE · STOCKBRIDGE, MA

Sabbath stews that Jewish cooks left to slowly simmer overnight inspired an invention that came to be the one and only Crock-Pot.

What a Crock

Slow-cooked meals were an early form of convenience food.

Rival introduced the Crock-Pot in 1971, and good timing was on its side: Within four years, the company made $93 million on sales of the device.

The Crock-Pot was based on a 1950s appliance—Naxon's Beanery—that primarily had one job: cooking legumes. Rival acquired the beanery's patent in 1970 and updated the device with Earth-inspired colors and a homey-sounding name. The Crock-Pot was sold with a book of recipes—from soup to cake—that showed the gadget's versatility.

The Crock-Pot went on the market as large numbers of women were joining the workforce.

Filling a pot with ingredients created a relatively low-effort dinner, and having a piping hot meal to serve after being away from the kitchen all day gave plenty of '70s women some level of work-life balance.

At the same time, an ongoing energy crisis was causing Americans to rethink their energy consumption. Leaving a Crock-Pot on for hours used less energy than an electric oven.

Fifty years on, the name Crock-Pot has remained synonymous with slow cookers—and they're still a hot item in the kitchen.

NATALIE WYSONG

Fast Facts on Slow Cookers
Dinner is served.

COUNTERTOP GADGET
Slow-cooking is more popular than ever. Even before sales of slow cookers doubled from 2000 to 2015, the majority of American households owned one, according to *Consumer Reports*.

....

MOTHER OF INVENTION
Irving Nachumsohn, later Naxon, learned the story of how his grandmother in the Jewish *shtetl* of Vilna, in Lithuania, made the stew called *cholent* for the Sabbath. On Friday evening, families brought their crocks of stew to the town bakery. The ovens' retained heat was enough to cook the cholent overnight. Naxon invented and patented an electric "beanery" that re-created the same low-and-slow cooking conditions.

....

RUN OUT OF STEAM
Slow cookers work at low temperatures, leveling out slightly below the boiling point. Steam accumulates, helping the cooking process along. Lifting the lid releases the trapped steam, prolonging the cooking time. Thus, the cardinal rule of slow-cooking: No peeking!

....

KILLER CROCK-POTS?
A faulty Crock-Pot's role in the death of a character on NBC's *This Is Us* in 2018 shocked fans, but slow cookers are actually one of the safest small appliances, drawing about as much current as an incandescent lightbulb. According to *Consumer Reports*, in the four-year span of 2012-2015, slow cookers caused only 103 fires, fewer than half of the 256 fires started by coffeemakers in the same time period.

....

FAIR PRICE
The price of the Crock-Pot has stayed steady since the first one was introduced at the National Housewares Show in Chicago. The basic models in a 4- to 5-quart size have always cost about $25.

RIVAL ARRIVES
The Rival Co. of Kansas City, Missouri, acquired Naxon's patent and set about broadening its market appeal. Professional recipe testers found that the pot could make a lot more than beans, and Rival packaged the renamed Crock-Pot with an 84-page cookbook. Within a few years, Rival improved on its own design by making the inner crock removable for easier cleaning.

....

EARTH TONES
Original Crock-Pots came in classic 1970s hues— Harvest, Avocado and Flame—with a brown crock inside the colorful casing. Now, the most popular finish is silver.

Naxon sold his patent for the cooker to Rival Co., which designed Crock-Pot's iconic look.

A PROUD PURCHASE
My mother, Mary Kirban, saved Green Stamps for a fox stole. Her mission accomplished, she happily wears it in the spring of 1970.
DOREEN MARY FRICK · ORD, NE

CLOTHES

» BRIGHT COTTONS

My aunt, schoolteacher Virginia Thurtle, second from right, and her friends dressed in sundresses for their last night in Hawaii during a vacation in the early 1950s.

MARY PALMER · VINEYARD HAVEN, MA

⌄ STILL A CLASSIC

I took this picture of my wife, Lea, in a crisp Chanel-style suit on a gorgeous hillside in California in 1945.

BILLY PEACOCK · ROARING SPRINGS, TEXAS

EASY TO SPOT

Gina, 2, Debbie, 4, and I wore ladybug dresses that my mother made for us. She also made dresses for herself, my sister and my niece.

JOANN SCHUELLER COOKE · PRESCOTT, AZ

☆ TOP OF THE DAY

I found this image among my uncle John Court's slide collection showing family and friends from about the late '30s to early '60s. These two women are staving off an autumn chill with stylish hats in the late 1940s.

CARL VINCENT •
MEDICAL LAKE, WA

» EAR CANDY

This is a photo of my mother from the mid-1950s. She's wearing a pair of clip-on earrings; a common accessory for women at the time.

TARA HOUGHTON •
DOROTHY, NJ

CHIC IN THE '70S

I found this image from 1977 of two women in the era's very popular fashions and colors: a peasant frock with ruffle trim, left, and a large-check polyester A-line dress in brown and rust.
ALBERT WAGNER

THE USA BY RAIL, BUS OR BOAT

Adventure at home via National Geographic.

1954 »

Steel Horse Views

Union Pacific Railroad had several all-in-one trips in 1954, including "Tour Z," which took in Bryce Canyon, Zion National Park and the Grand Canyon over 12 days. Cost for a Pullman coach was $281 —more than $2,700 today.

« 1954

Diesel Expeditions

Package tours on Greyhound Scenicruiser, with double-decker views, and Highland Cruiser (shown here) competed directly with rail— which in fact used buses to some destination points. Greyhound's 7-day Utah parks tour out of Los Angeles cost $163 in 1959. x

THE LURLINE **IS** HAWAII

Centers of Exciting Fun

to and from *Hawaii* on the *Lurline*

One of the liveliest fun-spots is the Pool . . . one of the most relaxing, a deck chair overlooking the vast blue sea . . . one of the brightest, the Dining Room for surpassing table delights . . . one of the gayest, the Veranda, for an evening of dancing. These and so many more centers of fun make your voyage overflow with pleasure. ■ Be sure to book round trip . . . the voyage back home has new diversions, new surprises. *It's twice the fun to sail the* LURLINE *both ways.* ■ See your Travel Agent or any Matson Lines office: New York, Chicago, San Francisco, Seattle, Portland, Los Angeles, San Diego, Honolulu.

THE LURLINE SAILS FROM SAN FRANCISCO AND LOS ANGELES ALTERNATELY

For the finest travel, the **LURLINE**...
for the finest freight service, the
Matson Cargo Fleet...to and from Hawaii

Matson Lines

1954   **Aloha Hawaii**

A mainstay of the Aloha State, Matson restored its venerable *Lurline* for passenger service out of San Francisco and Los Angeles in the mid-1950s. A trip on the Lurline usually ended with a stay at a Matson hotel in Waikiki. Matson exited the hotel business in 1959 to focus on container shipping.

Long before he was a household name, Barry Manilow sold household products with his jingles.

SING ALONG WITH JINGLES

MARKETERS KNOW WELL THE POWER of a good song. A catchy tune paired with punchy lyrics about a product can create a lasting earworm. While jingles have existed for as long as there have been radio and TV stations to play them, the advertising scene of 50-plus years ago was memorable for introducing some of the catchiest in history.

In 1971, McDonald's Corp. had a new commercial featuring seven guys cleaning the heck out of a restaurant and singing "You deserve a break today." Meanwhile,

Coca-Cola Co., ran a spot with people on a hilltop singing "I'd like to buy the world a Coke." And an insurance company promised, "Like a good neighbor, State Farm is there." A few notes of that last ditty still appear in State Farm commercials today. To think that a then-struggling singer-songwriter named Barry Manilow got paid just $500 for co-writing it.

Of course Manilow went on to a glittering music career, but he never forgot his early days as a jingle writer and performer. For years, his live shows included a medley of popular jingles—his own and others.

MARY-LIZ SHAW

Blender Still Cuts It

Young couple's splurge purchase
grows into reliable old friend.

When my husband, John, and I were expecting our first child in May 1961, we were 19 and 21 years old. John was stationed with the Air Force in California, and our monthly budget didn't allow for much more than the bare necessities.

We had heard about Oster blenders and agreed that if we had one, we could make our expected baby's food. It was expensive, but we would save money over time, so we bought it. I soon learned that the blender had many more uses in the kitchen than simply making baby food. New Oster owners could sign up to receive a recipe pamphlet once a month from the manufacturer. These were filled with blended-food ideas, and before long our blender became a much-loved—and much-used—appliance.

Years ago, Oster reissued its iconic beehive-style blender, similar to the one John and I bought. We didn't need to purchase the remake; our original Osterizer Deluxe was still going strong. That blender has served us without fail for 60 years. Though we scarcely could afford it in 1961, our Oster turned out to have been a bargain.

KATHY MANNEY · HENDERSON, NV

FOCUS ON: OSTERIZER

Founded in 1924 in Racine, Wisconsin, John Oster Manufacturing Co. introduced the Osterizer, with its beehive base and on/off toggle, in 1946 for about $40. Osterizers of all styles are quite popular on auction sites today, with some working models similar to Kathy's, which has two speeds, priced at around $50 or more.

John feeds David in 1961. The trusty Oster, above, was handy when David started on solid foods.

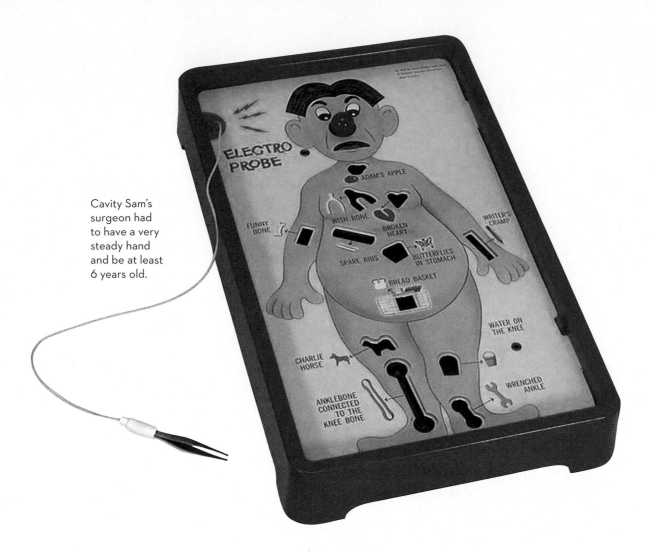

Cavity Sam's surgeon had to have a very steady hand and be at least 6 years old.

Is there a Fake Doctor in the House?

Operation gives surgery the silly treatment.

John Spinello was a student at the University of Illinois in 1962 when one of his design professors set an interesting assignment: Create a toy or a game.

"So I put this box together with the overcharged battery and the buzzer. And, by golly, it worked," Spinello remembers in the 2017 film Operation: Operation—The Power of Play.

Spinello showed his project to his godfather, a model-maker at Marvin Glass & Associates. The Chicago-based MGA developed some of the most successful games of the era, including Mouse Trap, Time Bomb, Simon, Mystery Date and Rock'em Sock'em Robots, under the very inventive eye of founder Marvin Glass.

Glass bought Spinello's concept for $500 and the promise of a job at graduation. Spinello didn't end up at MGA after graduating, but in 1965, his idea became Operation, one of the more unusual and enduring games of the '60s.

By now millions have performed surgery on the unfortunate Cavity Sam, whose spate of bizarre complaints—such as Water on the Knee, Butterflies in Stomach and Bread Basket—make up his "funatomy."

MICHELE WOJCIECHOWSKI

The Goofy Game for Dopey Doctors

OUT OF THE DESERT
Spinello's original game was set in Death Valley, and the object was to guide a character to water. Players moved an electric probe along a groove and into holes in a charged metal box. If the probe touched the sides of the groove or holes, it completed the circuit and a buzzer sounded.

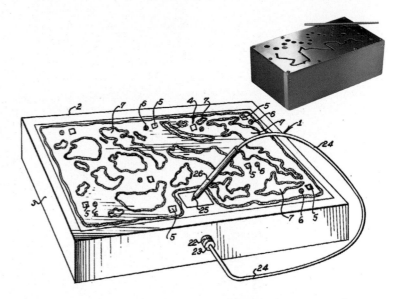

John Spinello created The Box that Sparked and Made Noise, top, for a design class in 1962. Above, a sketch for the 1965 patent filing for Death Valley, which later became Operation.

FANS GIVE BACK
Spinello (below) declared bankruptcy in 2008, which meant he couldn't afford $25,000 for oral surgery that he needed a few years later. His fellow game inventors Peggy Brown and Tim Walsh appealed to fans via a crowdfunding site, and raised enough money to pay for Spinello's operation and some of his other bills. Hasbro contributed by purchasing Spinello's original Death Valley prototype.

INSPIRING DESIGN
In a case of life imitating art, Andrew Goldstone, an ear, nose and throat doctor at Johns Hopkins, created a device for thyroid operations that alerts surgeons if they cut too close to the vocal cords. "It had to be floating around in my subconscious," Goldstone told Mental Floss in 2015, referring to Operation's buzzer setup. "But I didn't make the connection until later." His son made the link first: After Goldstone told him about the device, Alec Goldstone said, "You've reinvented Operation."

INTO THE HOSPITAL
Marvin Glass sold the rights to the prototype to Milton Bradley, where a designer named Jim O'Connor suggested making the game board a surgery patient and the probe a pair of tweezers.

FULL CIRCLE
Dr. Goldstone's invention was used when John Spinello's daughter Lisa had thyroid surgery. "Thanks, Dad," she says in the documentary about her father. "You saved my voice. Are you happy?" "Sometimes," Spinello quips.

NEW DIAGNOSIS
After remaining virtually unchanged since its introduction, the game of Operation got an update in 2004 in the form of a new illness for Cavity Sam. Hasbro, which bought Milton Bradley in 1984, had allowed fans to choose the ailment—Brain Freeze won with 54% of the vote. A 2013 game update, however, left fans pained. It featured a slimmed-down and younger Cavity Sam and wider openings that made it easier to remove game pieces.

Robin's mother saved these promo pieces, which hold happy memories of afternoon kids TV.

Bonkers for Bozo

Boyhood hero lives on with cherished collectibles.

B ack in the spring of 1976, when I was 4, I was devoted to the red-haired TV clown named Bozo. The term "superfan" was not in common use in the 1970s, but when it came to Bozo, that's what I was. My family got tickets to the show's Nashville taping as a special treat for me.

In the studio, producers sat the kids in a separate section of the audience. I was with my sister Cyndy, who was 10. The lights went down, the curtains parted and there was my idol! I yelled his name, then rushed the stage: "Bozo! Bozo! Bozo!" Production immediately halted. Cyndy heard the clown shout "Somebody get this kid out of here!"

The incident didn't wind up dampening my enthusiasm. I collected a lot of Bozo the Clown merchandise over the years. Once I outgrew my fascination for it, I sold it off at yard sales.

Fortunately, Mom packed away two of my Bozo towels so that I'd have some tokens of my childhood obsession. We found them in 2014 in a keepsake box. They're a fun reminder of that day in Nashville and of growing up in the 1970s. Bozo definitely was an important part of kids culture in that era.

ROBIN A. STONE · MURFREESBORO, TN

FOCUS ON: BOZO MEMORABILIA

Vintage Bozo the Clown merchandise is readily available on online auction sites. Talking Bozo dolls from the 1960s are offered at up to $75 for versions in good condition. Towels are rarer, and Robin's are in near-pristine shape, having been packed away for several years. Similar towels from the 1970s, but less fine than Robin's, were selling recently for up to $70 per item.

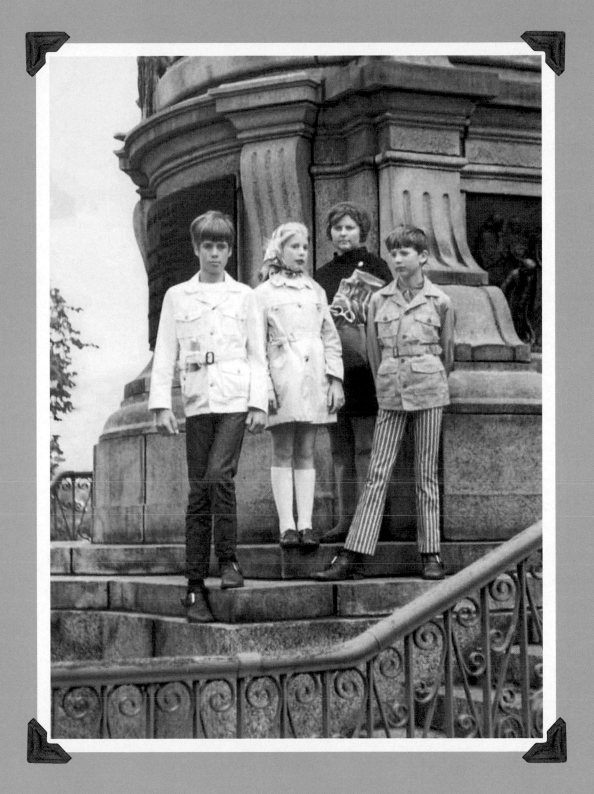

Mod Trip

Rick (right) and I wore those safari jackets everywhere in 1969, including
on a vacation to Canada, where we posed with our mom, Edythe, and
sister Debbie. And how about our hip high-top loafers?

BILL CRAFT · FORT RUSSELL, IL

CHAPTER 5

....

AT WORK

From early morning paper routes to a
surprising first day at the department
store, our jobs gave us plenty to
talk about and appreciate.

MAY · 55

Dropping off the *Reflector*

Charles Beaman, 14, delivers more than 100 copies of
The Daily Reflector to customers in Greenville, NC, in 1962.

Funny Money

Short-term job did the trick.

———

During my senior year at the University of Denver, I wanted to attend my fraternity's formal, a dressy event held at a nice resort outside Colorado Springs. I hadn't planned ahead, and so, naturally, I had hardly any money to cover my costs and buy a corsage for my date.

On the bulletin board in the student union, I saw that a new service station was opening across town. The company was hiring clowns for two shifts, so I went ahead and applied with one of my friends. Apparently we were the only ones to apply, and so we were both hired.

In the mid-'60s, a gas station opening was a big deal—attendants pumped the gas, checked the oil, washed the windshield and even checked the tire pressure. To celebrate the opening, customers got a set of engraved glasses when they filled up. The clowns' job was to stand in the middle of the busy street in front of the station, waving to people and displaying the beautiful glasses.

I arrived at the station ahead of time to prepare. The company provided the clown suit and makeup, which I applied in the station's bathroom. Putting on clown makeup is not nearly as easy as it sounds.

Without anyone to critique my makeup, I'm not sure I looked very jolly.

The first couple of hours were uneventful, except that the suit was hot, my feet ached and I felt like an idiot. With half my 6-hour shift left to go, a child approached. He was 8 or 9, and he watched me quietly for a few minutes, then said, "Hey, clown, do some tricks!"

"I don't know any tricks. Go away."

"Not until you do some tricks."

I glared at him and said, "Scram. Clowns can be mean, you know." That sent him scurrying, but I felt guilty about being mean to a little kid. I made myself concentrate on the money I'd make.

Around 9 p.m. the local teens began cruising. At first, it was enough for them to hurl insults and snide comments, but soon the sport became trying to hit the clown with a water balloon.

Finally, my shift ended. The service station operator thought the promotion had gone very well. "Would you be able to come back tomorrow?" he asked. I made the excuse that I would have to study and departed with my hard-earned reward.

JOHN BROADWELL · SENECA, SC

Work-Love Balance

Office friendship leads to marriage.

My small group of friends shared hobbies that I enjoyed, but when they headed to town for a night out, I usually preferred to stay home. Even after four years of college, I was shy and quiet. Looking to earn money for a master's degree program, I found a job in the stockroom at Buck Engineering in Spring Lake, New Jersey, in 1972.

After working there for almost a year and a half, I was promoted to inventory manager. I met frequently with my supervisor in the accounting office where Pam, a new accountant, had just been hired. Her halo of blond hair certainly attracted my attention, and the first time I saw her, I thought to myself that she could be "the one." It was very disappointing, then, to learn from one of my friends in the company bowling league that Pam was married. I put aside any thoughts of romance.

The inventory involved many late-night planning hours, but it went extremely well, even though it was my first time in charge. After the inventory was completed, the plant closed for a break at the end of the year. When we returned to work, my friend Jane met me in the stockroom with some very big news: Pam had decided to leave her bad marriage, and during the break had moved in with Jane.

Like me, Pam was quiet, but soon we began talking in the stockroom at work, and then we started dating. After the divorce was final, we were inseparable. Pam came to my company softball games, watched our lunchtime basketball games, and brought her knitting to the bowling alley.

Eighteen months later, in July 1975, I finally saved enough money to start classes for my master's degree in English and history at Trinity University in San Antonio. We loaded up Pam's car and headed to Texas. We got married at Trinity University's chapel in 1976. After I graduated, we headed back east, where our daughter, Stefanie, was born.

Pam and I were together for 42 years, until she died in December 2017. I'm thankful that I had the rare chance to find the love of my life.

TOM BARTH • FORT WASHINGTON, MD

Pam and Tom with daughter, Stefanie, in 1977.

Play Time Was Work Time

Made-up game was a child's version of the working man's routine.

During the 1940s, I lived the first seven years of my childhood on the south side of Pittsburgh. One of my favorite ways to enjoy myself was to play "working hard." I observed the hardworking men in my African American family and I wanted to be like them.

Our house was on Carson Street close to the Jones and Laughlin Steel Corp. mill, and very near the railroad tracks. The rough, grassy area near the track bed was peppered with rocks. Occasionally, there were also chips and lumps of coal that fell off uncovered train cars heading to the mill.

This busy, if dreary, industrial environment was my "place of work." I had to straighten it up! I asked my wonderful grandmother to pack me a lunch, as she faithfully did each morning for the men in the family. My lunch usually would consist of a sandwich sliced diagonally and maybe a cookie or a piece of fruit, each wrapped neatly in waxed paper and packed in a brown paper bag. I also would carry an ash shovel and an old galvanized bucket. Then off I went, walking with determination to meet and conquer my challenges of the day.

I would dig dirt and gather rocks, making neat piles. I also collected wood scraps for kindling and bits of coal chips or lumps for our kitchen stove.

After working what I called "my shift" for a while, I would break for lunch. Then it was back to work to finish my busy day. Eventually, tired and soiled, I walked home feeling pleased with myself.

Climbing the old wooden back steps of our timeworn house, I walked into our second-floor kitchen. There, with sincere pride, I proclaimed, "I'm home! I'm home!"

HARRY JAMES FORD · PITTSBURGH, PA

The view from the family porch shows the steel mill in the background. Above, Harry James at 5.

Two paperboys fold and tie their papers for delivery before starting their afternoon routes near Natchitoches, LA, in 1940.

Driving Duty Has Fringe Benefits

She masters manual shift, but, oh, that clutch isn't happy.

A s is the case with many paper routes, ours began when my brother Randy signed up for a bike route in the late 1960s in our village of Coloma, Wisconsin, to earn some extra cash. However, in our mostly rural area, Randy's job quickly escalated to a car route that involved the whole family, especially when winter rolled around.

Mom was most often tagged as chauffeur, with one of us kids riding shotgun, shooting a folded paper into the box next to the recipient's mailbox. But as each older kid signed up for driver's ed, we were also drafted for delivery duty. In many ways, that delivery duty was valuable for practicing driving skills.

Starting out, I was still getting the hang of shifting gears on our old Pontiac Catalina station wagon. It was a big clunky car and I learned very quickly just how close I could get to a newspaper box without hitting it. My brother Scott wasn't quite as adept as me; he once ran over a customer's fence while he was turning around in the unlucky lady's driveway.

My biggest difficulty was with the clutch, which I kept slipping. With all of those stops and starts, and the short distances between delivery points, that clutch got a major workout. We blew three of them before Dad finally acquired a second car for us to use to run errands and deliver newspapers.

It was a 1957 Chevy that Dad picked up through the school district where he worked. He fixed it up and painted it bright orange. We called it The Bomb, and had a great time showing it off to our friends. The only problem was the heater didn't work very well—I came home with frostbitten fingers and toes more than once after a winter paper-route run in The Bomb.

Fortunately, we all found better jobs by the end of high school and handed over the route to some other lucky person (or family).

I'm not sure what became of the Pontiac, but Dad traded in the orange Chevy for another '57 Chevy, which he painted bright red. We called that one The Cherry Bomb.

BRENDA HANSEN · CLINTONVILLE, WI

BLIZZARD? WHAT BLIZZARD?

IN THE EARLY 1950S, I HAD 129 CUSTOMERS on a residential route in Walkerton, Indiana, for the *South Bend Tribune*, which I delivered in the afternoon during the week and very early in the morning on Sundays.

One wintry Sunday, we waited but the papers didn't arrive at the usual drop-off, a bandstand near the post office. When my father called, he was told the trucks couldn't get out in the storm. So Dad drove the 20 miles into South Bend to pick up our bundles.

We had to load the papers on a sled to hand-deliver them in the storm, but all my customers got their papers by 11 a.m. that day.

Customers on other routes had to wait until the next day for their deliveries. We picked up a lot of new customers because of that.

We took good care of our customers and, as a result, we would get as much as $350 in tips and other gifts at Christmas. Walkerton was good to my family. I will always think highly of Walkerton and its people.

RALPH SMITH · NEW ALBANY, IN

Roland, 11, sells papers in Newark, NJ, in 1924. Child paper sellers were a common sight on city streets in the first part of the 20th century.

Jim poses with his 100-plus papers for a Christmas card in 1957.

FLEXING HIS FINANCIAL MUSCLE

THIS WAS A SPECIAL TIME in my life. I started as a carrier for The *San Bernardino Sun-Telegram* when I was 13. I was proud to be named Carrier of the Year in 1957. I sometimes gave my girlfriend a ride on the handlebars as I delivered papers. I also chipped a tooth holding the newspaper bag in my mouth by its metal ring.

We earned extra money by going "sub hunting"—selling subscriptions door to door—then used the earnings as points to buy items out of a catalog. I got bongo drums and a transistor radio that way. And I won a badminton set as carrier of the year.

Gee whiz, it felt good. I had the power to purchase whatever I chose. My carrier friends and I would buy muscle tees or collared shirts from Lang's Menswear. Boy, we looked cool, daddy-o.

Or so we thought.

JIM VANCE · TUSTIN, CA

HEY, WANNA TRADE?

I LIED AND SAID I WAS 12 (I WAS REALLY 10)
to get my *Long Island Press* route in Queens, New York, in 1947. I did it for six years, opting for larger and larger routes each time.

Many houses in Queens neighborhoods were for two families, which meant learning to do double-barreled paper flips onto the steps while riding by.

My favorite stop wasn't a customer in the traditional sense. The route concluded at the rear entrance of a commercial bakery, where a baker would grab a fresh loaf—ah, I can smell it now!—off the conveyor belt to trade for that day's paper.

RICHARD STERN · NEW BERN, NC

IMPROVING MY BUSINESS ACUMEN!

I TOOK OVER A *TOLEDO TIMES* MORNING ROUTE
in the '40s that originally had 69 customers but had shrunk to 20. I went to every canceled customer and asked why they'd quit the paper. All said that it came too late to read before work.

So I offered a deal: I would deliver the paper by 6 a.m. every day or they didn't have to pay. The next week I was delivering 69 papers. For as long as I had that route, I was late only once–and all insisted on paying anyway.

I liked getting up early. In summer I'd time the start so I was heading into the sunrise.

I still enjoy Toledo sunrises.

LEWIS KUJAWSKI · TOLEDO, OH

EARLY MORNING ROUTE OFFERS PEACE AND QUIET

WHEN OUR FAMILY OF NINE
moved from Pennsylvania to Indiana in the late 1940s, Dad wanted me, the eldest child at 12, to learn self-sufficiency. So I got a paper route.

As far I know, I was the only female carrier delivering the morning *Indianapolis Star* and the evening *News* on the city's east side then. I had an average of 50 customers for three years. I preferred the afternoon deliveries, although it was calming to be out walking at 6 a.m. with so few people and almost no traffic.

I was always careful to put the paper where the customer wanted it, and would never think of tossing it!

LOUISE ROBERTSON MARKVE
BUFFALO, MN

Once, as a carrier for the Burlington County Times, I won a 24-cup coffee maker; 50 years later, we still use it.

ROBERT J. MILLER
MOUNT LAUREL, NJ

A boy sells papers in front of a Georgia general store in 1938.

Extra Training Unlocks the Job

Considerate manager spots key employee.

We lived on the poor side of town in East Moline, Illinois. Dad was often out of work, but my mother did the best she could with the little money he earned. Eventually, Dad started his own trash-collecting business, which earned a decent income.

At United Township High School, I took my first key-punch class, which I really loved. After I graduated, I took a six-week course and earned a key-punch certificate.

Two large farm equipment companies were important employers in the area. I first applied at International Harvester Co., where the interviewer laughed and told me to come back when I had experience. I found out through the grapevine that John Deere needed a key-punch operator in the accounting department. I put on my best dress and went to meet with James Downing, the head of the department. During the interview, he asked me what my father's profession was. I hesitated, since I was embarrassed to say that my father picked up trash. After I told him, he politely proceeded.

Then—lo and behold—he said, "Welcome to the accounting department."

There was another hurdle: When I was signing the paperwork for the position, I saw employees had to be at least 18—my birthday was just two weeks away! Jim consulted with someone in the employment department, and told me they'd hold the position.

True to their word, on my birthday in September 1968, they called and asked if I still wanted the job. And that wasn't all: During my interview, Jim had learned that I didn't have a car, so I would have to take cabs and the bus to and from work. Jim arranged for me to carpool with a co-worker. I paid the driver each and every week until I saved up enough to buy a car.

I held various positions in my 30-year career at John Deere, and I retired in 2000. I never forgot that it was possible because one man gave a shy girl a chance.

GINNY WOMACK HOWARD · LAKE CITY, FL

Small Town, Big Returns

Paper route starts with the comics
and ends with a cool ride.

W e lived in a delightful town, Shell Beach, in San Luis Obispo County on the central California coast. Mom and Dad bought their first home and paid $60 a month on the mortgage. I don't know why I should remember that, except in the early '60s it was a large payment for them. They didn't need my financial help, but seeing them committed to their obligation instilled in me a good work ethic.

I signed up for Little League, but then I heard about a chance to deliver the newspaper. For me, it wasn't a hard choice. I was a klutz at sports with little hope of improving, so I become a paperboy.

The Tribune of San Luis Obispo was an afternoon paper and I soon got into a routine. I'd come home from school to a stack of about 40 papers. I would read the comics quickly, then roll up each paper, secure it with a rubber band and pack the bundles in a cloth bag on my bike's handlebars. My route was about 3 miles and took around 45 minutes.

I was proud of my throwing technique. I could toss the rolled paper so that it would walk end over end right up the porch and land at the front door. Once, a customer claimed I'd broken his screen door. To this very day I question whether I did, but Dad sided with the customer. So as a good businessman, I paid for the repair.

Collecting was a chore that I never wanted to do alone. I used to bribe my friend David to go with me by first taking him to the corner store for a pie or candy.

The Tribune sent me a bill every month; whatever was left over after I collected $1.75 from each customer was my salary— about $30 a month. I saved most of it and built up a pretty fair account.

One day I was sitting with a friend on the front porch when a pickup truck rolled by with a Suzuki 200 cc dirt bike on the bed.

I joked about the driver stopping at my place with that, but it kept moving.

A few minutes later, the pickup was back, and this time it did turn into our driveway. I was certain the pickup driver had made a mistake, but the bike truly was mine.

My father found it on sale and bought it with my route savings. I sure didn't mind, but there was a problem: I couldn't get a license for it because I wasn't 16 yet. For a few months, I had to be content with loading it into Dad's pickup and having him take me to an off-road field to ride.

These were wonderful experiences. I learned about responsibility, serving customers and how to manage money. As an adult, I became a store manager for a major company, where I used many of the skills I learned as a paperboy.

JOHN MOYER · MCALESTER, OK

Two paperboys relax in front of a barber shop in Rockport, MA, in 1949.

Mom Was a Stripper

At pennies an hour, a good attitude was a fringe benefit.

———

Shirley, my mom, grew up in an agricultural area of Michigan. In the 1960s, our family was traveling to visit her parents when she pointed out the car window and said, "Look, kids! That's where I used to strip!"

For one brief moment, I thought our ordinary family might be more interesting than my adolescent imagination had ever dreamed. There were absolutely no pirates or bigamists or bank robbers in my family tree—nothing beyond a way-back ancestor whose father may have been a fly-by-night traveling salesman. But a stripper? At last, this was gossip worthy of sharing with all my friends!

When almost all the able-bodied young men were overseas defending our country during World War II, farmers often hired young women as laborers to replace the workmen. In Michigan, the local apple orchards had to be thinned of small apples in a process called stripping. That was it, and though the reality was anticlimactic, it showed Mom's flair for telling a funny story.

In addition to stripping apple trees, my mom spent a summer hoeing a neighbor's cornfields. It was hot, boring, backbreaking work, for which she and the other young laborers earned just a bit more than their age: 12½ cents per hour.

Sometimes when the farmer was not around, the children held amateur talent shows or put on impromptu plays in the fields. One day Mom turned her hoe upside down and pretended that it was a microphone. While my mom belted out "Somewhere Over the Rainbow" in her best Judy Garland impersonation, she looked up to see her employer glaring at her in disapproval of this frivolous waste of his wages. Mom turned her hoe around and got back to work.

Mom stayed home to raise us five kids, then went to work when we were all in school. She was a cashier at the local grocery store, referring to herself as the Chubby Checker.

Mom always left an impression. Many years after she worked for the farmer, Mom's sister, a nurse, was caring for him. My aunt asked him if he remembered my mom. After a moment, he recalled his 12½-cent-wage earner and gruffly replied, "Hmmph! I overpaid your sister."

When I heard these stories, I gained a new respect for the teenage version of my mom, who was willing to hoe a crabby penny-pinching farmer's corn in the hot sun for meager wages—and even then, she still felt like singing.

Mom had a wonderful, sometimes risque, sense of humor, and she didn't hold it back. To this day, I'm very grateful that she passed it on to us.

DENISE THIERY · ALEXANDRIA, KY

Shirley entertained her kids with hilarious versions of events. Here she is as a teen in the early 1940s (left and above.)

In the Spotlight

Big-city job kept young graduate on her toes.

When I graduated from high school in Mount Hope, West Virginia, in 1966, many of the students had their futures already planned. Some of my classmates' parents could afford to send them to college, and some boys were drafted and went to Vietnam. For girls, we had few options besides teaching and nursing, and many opted to get married and start families. But none of those things were for me.

After a long job search, I found work at a dry cleaners. I made 75 cents an hour and knew that men made more. One year later, after saving every penny I could gather, I was on a Greyhound bus headed to Chicago, Illinois.

Being from the country, I found the huge city quite overwhelming at first. I moved into an apartment and got a job at Maybelline, which was headquartered in Chicago. I worked there for a year, then I was ready to move on.

I found a good job at another well-known Chicago firm, Bell & Howell. The company was known for its audiovisual technology—home movie cameras, projectors, tape recorders and instant

Donna looked
to Chicago for
career adventure,
and she found it.

I saw my new supervisor
and his boss coming toward me.
I thought, "It was nice working
here for half a day."

cameras. I was very excited to be hired as an inspector in the home movie department, which paid very well.

I started my new job on a warm April day—a no-jacket day. New to the routines of my workplace, I skipped lunch and went outside. No one was around, and I leaned against a car to enjoy the spring sunshine.

Suddenly I saw my new supervisor and his boss coming toward me. I thought, It was nice working here for half a day.

They were carrying a large movie camera and a microphone, and my supervisor instructed me to talk into the microphone while they recorded me. It seemed as if all I said was "Blah blah blah," but I did manage to talk about how nice the weather was that day.

When they finished recording me, they explained they had a new prototype of a sound home movie

camera—it was a video camera. Their recording of me was for a demonstration of the new product. After they thanked me and left, I felt only a deep sense of relief that I hadn't been fired on my first day after all.

A month or so later, I learned that my recording turned out well—the new cameras were popular—and I received a generous bonus in my paycheck as a thank-you.

I loved living in Chicago—it was a great place to work, and I always found something new to explore. Eventually, I got married and had two children, a daughter and son. But the adventure of working and living on my own in the city, when such a life was not quite as acceptable for a single woman as it is now, has always given me a satisfying sense of pride and independence.

DONNA McGUIRE TANNER · OCALA, FL

STEPPING OUT

Do you remember playing dress-up in Mom's heels or loafing around in Dad's shoes? Take a walk through these styles.

Luxury, At Last

After World War II, millions of middle-class Americans were able to purchase the luxurious clothing and accessories that had been restricted during the war effort. These ritzy leather designs were no exception.

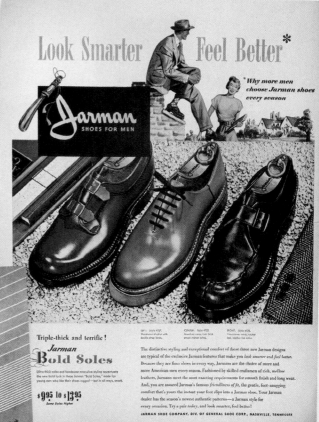

Predescessor to Stilettos

These slingback heels came out just before stilettos burst onto the scene in the early '50s. Until then, designers had lacked the technology necessary to make the heel tall and slim—and, importantly, still able to bear the weight of a full-grown woman.

1951   **No Wear to Go**

It might seem surprising now, but there once was a time when shoe-sole companies put out ads. This one boasts that Avonite Soles give two to three times the wear of leather—it's no wonder they earned the seal of approval from the Girl Scouts.

EARLY BIRD OR SLEEPYHEAD?

Whichever you were, scrumptious breakfast treats made you linger at the table.

1958 »

Slimming and Satisfying
This brightly colored ad by Post cereal promises readers—and women in particular—slim waistlines, lovely fashions and envious looks if they choose to start their day with a bowl of Grape-Nuts..

"Any protein cereal helps keep you the right size...as long as it's **Post Grape-Nuts**"

Post GRAPE-NUTS *Post*

SIZE 10

DICK SARGENT

Automatic

NOW! All you do is drop in the bread
Bread lowers itself **automatically**, which turns on current
When perfectly toasted, current turns off **automatically**
Toast raises itself silently, without popping or banging

No levers to push

By the makers of *Sunbeam* MIXMASTER

« 1952

Hands-Free and Silent
Sunbeam highlights its brand-new toaster in this ad; with features such as automatically lowering bread (no need for levers!) and raising the toast without noisy "popping" or "banging," Sunbeam's offering combines updated technology with added convenience.

⩔ 1948

A Heavenly Morning

Chase and Sanborn Coffee set out to make "angels" out of grouchy non-morning people. Advertising their new blend as a "spirit-lifting success," it promises an easier, cheerier wake-up for all.

1956 »

The Promise of Pancakes

Table Products Co. encourages its consumers to eagerly await the next dawn... as long as it offers "petal-light pancakes with a generous topping of Sleepy Hollow Syrup." Who needs dinner when breakfast is so sweet?

Paper carriers like Charles Beaman, 14, left, and Denny Mayer, often met many interesting people on their daily routes.

Treasures Hidden in Plain Sight

Carrier collects new friends and lifelong lessons.

My dad's cousins Ruth and Ty Mayer owned one of two newsstands in Crestline. I started delivering papers for them in 1963, when I was 10 years old.

I was one of several carriers. We delivered newspapers from the neighboring towns of Mansfield, Galion and Bucyrus, and a few of our customers took the two Columbus newspapers.

We started each delivery day folding the papers in the garage on a long counter or side table, standing on wooden soda pop crates to be at the right height. We folded papers in squares, triples or longs, depending on the thickness. I do not recall any carrier reading a paper before folding it.

Part of the enjoyment of the job was socializing with the other carriers. On days when newspapers were late getting to the newsstand, we found creative ways to occupy ourselves—like snowball fights in winter. It frazzled Ruth Mayer's nerves. She was talented at showcasing her emotions.

As a ballplayer, I was pretty accurate with my throws, but I dented the odd aluminum door and tossed a paper or two onto the roof. Oops! But I learned early on that if you treated your customers well, they were generous at Christmastime. Even throughout the year, several customers routinely gave me cookies or candy when I came by. The Oliphants served me hot chocolate as I warmed up inside their home on very wintry days.

Mr. Walker owned a gas station that became my regular pit stop. I'd buy a pop and a candy bar and sit down for a visit with him and his dog Lucky.

My most interesting customer was a resident in our local nursing home. I called her Grandma Gardner. She always looked forward to my arrival and I very much enjoyed seeing her. Her 100th birthday was a special day—she was the toast of the nursing home.

One day I entered Grandma Gardner's room and her bed was empty. A nurse took me aside and broke the news that Grandma Gardner had died. She was 104. That was my saddest day on the route. I always remember her birthday—March 4.

My newspaper days are some of my best memories. My customers were kind; they helped me understand how special older people are to children. I'm very grateful to my cousins for giving me the opportunity to work for them for five years. The job taught me to be responsible and to be considerate of others. It is rather sad that in today's world, paperboys are no longer necessary.

DENNY MAYER · CRESTLINE, OH

Earning the Daily Bread

Dad delivered while Mom saved.

For much of the early 20th century, homemakers could expect to see three delivery professionals at their doors—the mailman, the milkman and the bread man.

My dad, Alphonse Poyant, worked for My Bread Baking Co. in New Bedford during that time. He made door-to-door deliveries of bread—nothing fancy, nothing artisan—climbing up many flights of stairs at the apartment buildings we called double- and triple-deckers in the city's north end.

During the Great Depression, many of my dad's customers simply could not afford the 5 to 10 cents that paid for a loaf. Being a kind and generous man, he was usually able to work out a payment plan for those customers. If a family was in dire straits, Dad used money from his own pocket on the family's behalf.

Dad's routine started early each morning. He owned a wagon, which he loaded with the day's bread before hitching it to the bakery's horse. After checking his books, he'd begin navigating the day's route, which the horse knew without any direction from Dad. Even though the horse was self-guided, Dad longed for the day when he would have a "horseless carriage"— a delivery truck.

One day, Dad learned that his company was selling one of its trucks for $400. The price may as well have been a $1 million. But my mom, Rhea, had a secret during those Depression years.

Without telling Dad, my ever-frugal mom had gone ahead and opened her own savings account at the Merchants National Bank. For some time, she'd been making regular deposits, some of which were less than a dollar!

Dad's pining for a truck he could never afford pulled at Mom's heartstrings. One night, Mom presented her bankbook to

Dad, showing him the account with a balance of more than $400.

Besides being our breadwinner, Dad was a winner in many other ways as well, including marrying an unselfish wife who showed that it pays to save your pennies!

SUSAN POYANT • NEW BEDFORD, MA

Alphonse delivered bread in New Bedford. Here, Rhea stands next to him, with a triple-decker in the background.

Hanky-Panky

Teen clerk gets more than she bargained for on her first day.

R.J. Goerke department store in Elizabeth, New Jersey, billed itself correctly as "the fashion center of Union County."

The six-story department store had a teen fashion board made up of area high school girls. I represented Cranford High School.

We met monthly with the buyer for junior dresses and sportswear, and discussed fashion trends. One trend was wearing wool Bermuda shorts to sporting events during the winter, with our coats flying wide open. We froze—but we were trendy.

As my 16th birthday neared, I applied for a part-time sales position to work after school on Thursday nights and Saturdays. It was easy to get the job since they already knew me. My birthday fell on a Thursday, and I raced from school to the personnel office. They sent me to handkerchiefs —a department with a staff of one—to fill in for someone who called in sick. I confidently made my way across the store to my station.

The department was located right beside the front door. It had a glass counter filled with beautifully displayed handkerchiefs, which were samples of the complex patterns embroidered with delicate French knots. The supply of handkerchiefs was stored in drawers on the wall behind the counter. On top of the glass counter was a basket filled with plastic rain caps.

I was at my post only about 10 minutes when a small grandmotherly woman approached. I greeted her with the standard "Hello, may I help you?" She looked into the case and pointed to several handkerchiefs that she wanted to see. I thought it best not to disturb the display in the case, so I turned around to take the designs she wanted from the drawers.

Suddenly, the quiet of the elegant store was interrupted by some wild noises behind me—unbelievable grunts and scuffling!

I turned around to see my customer on the floor wrestling with the store detective! He had spotted her quickly scooping plastic rain hats into her umbrella while my back was turned and tackled her.

The overzealous store detective, who was a retired prison guard, took his job very seriously and didn't hesitate to subdue the little old lady before taking her to an office for whatever her fate held. I was rattled by my awkward entrance into the working world and the loss of my very first sale.

CAROL ELY · ROSELAND, VA

R.J. Goerke's teen fashion board helped the department store stay on trend. On the previous page, Carol models a plaid dress and hat.

Phil loved shopping with wife, Roz.

SATISFIED CUSTOMERS

ROSALIND, MY NEW BRIDE, AND I PACKED UP and left New York City to start our life together in 1972. Williamsport, Pennsylvania, had a vibrant downtown with an open-air fish market, a shop that roasted coffee and peanuts and the elegant L.L. Stearns & Sons department store, where a cup of coffee at the lunch counter was five cents, with a 100% tip being the local custom.

L.L. Stearns' clerks still wrapped purchases using paper and spooled string. Mostly lifelong employees, they were knowledgeable specialists in their departments. Buying window shades for our new apartment was a pleasant experience, with the clerk demonstrating various room-darkening materials. The book clerks were as well-read as those in the independent bookstore a couple of blocks away.

Full-service department stores made one feel special just being there.

PHIL LIEBERMAN · SARASOTA, FL

Suddenly, the quiet of the elegant store was interrupted by wild noises behind me.

Pete and son Joe behind the counter at Matz's Confectionery.

Small-Town Candy Man

Hard worker had the right touch for a sweet business.

Pietro Mazza, my grandfather, was born in Italy. But he proudly displayed his love for his new country with a tattoo of the Statue of Liberty on his left forearm. In 1923, he moved his family to Vicksburg, Michigan, to be close to the family of his wife, Marietta. There, Peter Matz, as he was known, opened Matz's Confectionery, a sandwich, ice cream and candy shop.

Customers loved his tin roof sundaes and banana splits, but best of all were his homemade candies: caramels, brittles and taffy. He cooked his candies in a copper kettle, and then poured the hot mixture onto a marble surface to cool. Pete even invented a machine that spread the hot candy to an even thickness. Unfortunately, he never patented his useful invention.

Since childhood, Pete worked hard, first as a shoeshine boy, then rolling steel at Simmons Bedding Co. to make beds for the troops and finally at his shop. He spent hours shining the containers that held his homemade syrups, cleaning the floors and hosing down the sidewalk in front of his store each morning.

On a fall day in 1929, after Pete made a routine bank deposit, the bank closed. He never saw that money again. The years that followed were rough, and bills he was owed went unpaid. But Matz's Confectionery survived, and eventually his son Joe joined him in the business.

When Pete died, it was the end of an era. He was remembered for his honesty and generosity, including the ice cream treats he donated to local sports teams and new mothers at Franklin Memorial Hospital.

He was the kind of grandfather who lives in a girl's heart, even when she's all grown up and is a grandma herself.

MARY ANN HAYWARD · VICKSBURG, MI

The Morning Route

I was the proud *San Bernardino Sun-Telegram* Carrier of the Year in 1957.
Working as a carrier was a very special time in my life.

JIM VANCE · TUSTIN, CA

CHAPTER 6

OUR HEROES

From the battlefields to training at the base, our heroes gave us much to be grateful for—and admire.

Who Could It Be?

My father, Dr. Hugh Hickey, always said the character of Hot Lips on
*M*A*S*H* was based on a real person, but he would never say if she was
shown in this photo he took of his unit's nurses.

DAVE HICKEY · WAUKESHA, WI

Doctor for a Night

Reassuring letter recalls comforting bedside manner.

My stepfather, Al Moyer, was very brave to marry a widow with three small children. I know that for a fact, because I was his new 6-year-old daughter, and I was trouble with a capital "T"!

In time, though, he and I developed a special bond. I felt privileged and honored to help care for him when he became ill near the end of his life. We looked through his photo albums and letters, and he told me about his time serving in the military.

Alfred Frederick Moyer Sr. was barely 17 when he landed at Peleliu with the Marines during World War II. Later, he served in Korea. That was where he had a very harrowing experience.

Temporarily off the front line, Dad was pitching in wherever he could. He was helping care for a wounded Marine who'd been burned with phosphorus. During the night, the Marine was in great pain, and Dad gave him a dose of morphine: He didn't know that each vial contained two doses, and he injected the entire tube. In the morning, he discovered his mistake, and spent several hours worrying, as the injured Marine still was not awake.

After 18 hours, his patient finally began to stir, to Dad's great relief. That particular serviceman, David King, wrote many years later, calling Dad, affectionately, "Dr. Moyer": "I want to thank everyone for occasionally checking my pulse to see to it that I was still among the living...people who were not there simply wouldn't believe the spirit of community that we all shared in order to exist..."

Al Moyer served in both World War II and the Korean War.

All Dad shared of what he had seen and endured helped me to understand his work ethic, integrity and determination. I am proud to call him Dad.

KIM BABCOCK · CHITTENANGO, NY

"People who were not there simply wouldn't believe the spirit of community that we all shared."

Kumiko and Joseph married in 1951, before the law changed to allow her to enter the U.S. They were together 68 years until her death in late 2019.

Peace and then Love

Two hearts find each other in Occupied Japan.

It was April 1947, and it was cherry blossom time in Japan. I was with the 24th Infantry stationed at Camp Chickamauga in Beppu, Kyushu. We maintained athletic and recreational facilities for the occupying troops and their dependents.

One of my duties was assisting in the operation of the Lanik Theater, which was a former Japanese opera house. During a standard walk-around of the theater one afternoon, I noticed a pair of Japanese clogs, called geta, by one of the exit doors. Since it is Japanese custom to remove geta or shoes when entering a building, I assumed an unauthorized person had entered the theater. I searched, but after about 15 minutes found no one. I got back to the exit to find the geta gone.

About a week later, I saw the geta again by the same door. Once more I searched the theater and came up empty-handed, but when I got to the exit, I saw a Japanese girl rapidly walking away down the lane.

In my best phrase-book Japanese, I called out to her, "Ano ne ojosan! Doko ikimasu ka?" ("Hey, girl! Where are you going?") She took one look at me and ran off. I was surprised at how fast a person could run while wearing geta.

A few days later I saw her again. This time I tried to be more polite. "Chotto matte kudasai!" ("Please wait!") She stopped, and we had a broken Japanese-English conversation.

I learned that her name was Kumiko and that she was working as a cook and housemaid for Lt. John J. Rock and his wife, Jean, who taught at the school for children of dependents. Kumiko had been coming to the theater to get help from one of the interpreters. She needed several American recipes that Jean Rock had given her translated into Japanese.

I asked Kumiko for a date, but she refused. At that time, any fraternization between American service personnel and Japanese women was strongly discouraged. But thankfully, after seeing her from time to time at the theater over the next month, I finally persuaded her to have a date with me. We met at the home of a friend of the Japanese interpreter.

That date was the beginning of our romance and led to our marriage of more than 68 years, four children, seven grandchildren, and, at the time of this writing, eight great-grandchildren.

JOSEPH NEGRELLI · MENTOR, OH

TOWARD VICTORY

Vintage ads encouraged civilians to keep soldiers on their minds and in their hearts.

1943 »

Sending Love—and Chocolate

Whitman's modified its slogan in this 1943 ad, saying "A soldier never forgets the folks who remember." It encourages readers not only to send samplers, but also to send letters to let him know he's missed and thought of often.

« 1944

Hushed Moments

This 1944 ad imagines what it would be like to be among soldiers traveling toward ships that took them overseas— drawing deep breaths, holding letters and wondering if they can make final telephone calls. These, it says, are the sights Pennsylvania Railroad workers see every day.

© 1943, The Studebaker Corporation

"You purr just like those engines Dad builds!"

They're Studebaker-built Wright Cyclones for the famous Boeing Flying Fortress

SOLDIER HARRY RYAN and his father were fellow craftsmen in the Studebaker factory prior to Pearl Harbor.

They comprised one of the many father-and-son teams that have been a unique Studebaker institution since the business was founded in 1852.

Today, all over the world, large numbers of young men who once were Studebaker craftsmen, are engaged in using military equipment instead of building it.

In many instances, their fathers, and other older members of their families, are producing Flying Fortress engines, multiple-drive military trucks and other war matériel in the busy Studebaker plants.

For generations, one family after another in Studebaker's home community has maintained a tradition of Studebaker employment. This has resulted in a quality of craftsmanship unmatched in the automotive world.

That craftsmanship is now being utilized to the limit, on behalf of our Nation and its Allies, in the production of large quantities of military equipment. And it will provide finer Studebaker motor cars and motor trucks than ever before for civilian use, after victory comes.

STUDEBAKER

Builder of Wright Cyclone engines
for the Boeing Flying Fortress, big multiple-
drive military trucks and other
vital war matériel

"Always give more than you promise"
That Studebaker watchword has been faithfully observed for more than 20 years by craftsman Henry C. Ryan. Today he is helping to build Wright Cyclone engines for the Flying Fortress in one of Studebaker's aircraft engine plants. On some not-too-distant tomorrow, he and his soldier son, Harry, hope to be building Studebaker cars again for you.

1943 — A Different Kind of Purr

Studebaker provided Wright Cyclone engines for the Boeing Flying Fortress, as well as military trucks and, as the ad reads, "other vital war materials." While it noted that many of its workers were fighting rather than in the factories, it kept readers' spirits up by promising Studebaker craftsmanship would return in trucks and motor cars for everyday use "when victory comes."

Harvey saw action in multiple major battles during WWII.

A Cup of Strong English Tea

War held horrors, but this GI chose
to remember some good things.

Four of my Grandmother Margaret's siblings fought in World War II. One of them, Harvey Hudson, served as a a truck driver in an engineer battalion. Uncle Harvey's service began in North Africa, then he went to Sicily, and later he went to central Europe and England. Notably, my uncle fought at Normandy and in the Battle of the Bulge.

While fighting during D-Day, Uncle Harvey stopped his truck and got out; the soldier driving the truck behind him pulled ahead into Uncle Harvey's spot, and he was killed by an explosion. Uncle Harvey witnessed many other horrifying things during his service, but when he talked to me about his time overseas, he mainly focused on the good memories.

Uncle Harvey recalled with a smile the people and the wonderful food in Italy, and told me one happy story about his time stationed in England. He was being served tea in someone's home in the countryside.

He needed to wait for what seemed like an eternity before he was allowed to drink his tea, because English tea was steeped for much longer than he was used to at home.

After the war, miraculously, he and all of his brothers had returned home safely, and Uncle Harvey went on to have eight children and many grandchildren and great-grandchildren.

His heart was always partly in Nova Scotia, his father's birthplace, where he owned a parcel of land. He would regale us with his tales of the ceilidhs—the traditional gatherings—he attended there over the years.

Uncle Harvey was a talented carpenter, and he built the kitchen of my childhood home. He was a lover of animals and good food, and was a fantastic storyteller. He told me many of those stories while sitting in his recliner with his beloved pup, Louis, in his lap.

He was my grandmother's last living sibling. He died in 2018, just 22 days shy of his 100th birthday. His passing marked the loss of a great man, and the end of an era for our family. I'm thankful I got to learn about the remarkable life that he led.

MEGAN BRENNAN · BEVERLY, MA

In Japan After the War

GI witnessed life in Kobe restart amid wreckage.

A fter the war ended in 1945, the Allies began a military occupation of Japan, which lasted until 1952. I was part of the forces stationed there, serving in the U.S. Army in Kobe. I worked at a medical supply warehouse that employed several Japanese workers.

One of our assigned tasks was flying medical supplies to areas that had been devastated by the war, such as Iwo Jima, Guam, Okinawa, Korea and the Philippines. Brig. Gen. Robert W. Crichlow, who was in charge of Kobe Base, ordered me to personally deliver supplies to Seoul, Korea, on a fighter plane. I still have the original orders issued by General Crichlow for the assignment.

While in Japan, I saw Mount Fuji and also took a day trip to Nagasaki, the site of the second atomic bomb strike. From the train, I could see that the rice fields were full of downed Japanese fighter planes called Zeros. As for the bomb site, there really wasn't much to see: Within a mile of ground zero, everything was annihilated.

During my time in Kobe, Japan, experienced a major earthquake. On Dec. 20, 1946, I was asleep in my quarters on the fifth floor of an old building. I was awakened by shaking, and I looked outside to see the buildings opposite me swaying. People in various degrees of dress were running through the streets, and everyone in my building began to run down the stairs to get outside. No one dared use the elevator. The earthquake was a magnitude 8.1, and 1,362 people died.

Despite all the tragedy that I saw around me, I have warm memories of the wonderful Japanese people I met during my service. They were all very friendly and sincere, and showed no animosity toward us. They were ordinary people, just like us.

We were not allowed to fraternize with Japanese employees at the medical depot, nor were we allowed to visit Japanese businesses or residences. However, we were allowed to visit a dance hall.

One of the men who worked in the office invited me to his home. Permissible or not, I went. He introduced me to his wife and we sat on the floor. Now, I think back often to the life-changing experience of my time in Japan.

MALCOLM FIFE · FOUNTAIN RUN, KY

Malcolm's co-worker, in dark jacket at right, invited him to his home. Malcolm is in the back row, center.

TALES FROM BOOT CAMP

NEW LOOK

Early in 1973, I took my first flight ever, to the Marine Corps Recruit Depot in San Diego, California.

A receiving drill instructor met us as we exited the bus and ran toward the yellow footprints that indicated where to go for processing.

One step in the process was getting a haircut. At the age of 17, I was very proud of my free-flowing shoulder-length hair, which the drill instructor spotted. Comparing me to a well-known Bible figure, he said, "Come here!" I got into the chair and the barber asked how I wanted my hair cut. Naively, I said, "I have a lot of split ends—could you make them all even?"

He put the clippers in the middle of my forehead and said, "No problem." In a few minutes, every hair on my head was less than 1/8 inch long. "There," he said, "Now it's all even."

DALE A. HAAG • MONTGOMERY, TX

By the end of training, Joanne's uniform was squared away.

AT EASE AT LAST

Basic training at Lackland Air Force Base in San Antonio, Texas, in 1974 consisted of six grueling weeks of classroom studies, physical training and hot weather so that we could become airmen in uniform. At the screech of the 5 a.m. alarm, raw recruits hurled themselves out of bed with 15 minutes to get ready, including making a bed with covers tight enough to bounce a coin.

Our days were filled with someone barking orders at us to salute, stand at attention and straighten the "gig line" of our clothing, with every other command a corrective action. Several weeks into the training, my parents, Emily and O.A. Walker, came to visit on family day—it was delightful to see friendly faces.

All recruits, including Dale, got the same treatment.

JOANNE CLAYTON • HERRIN, IL

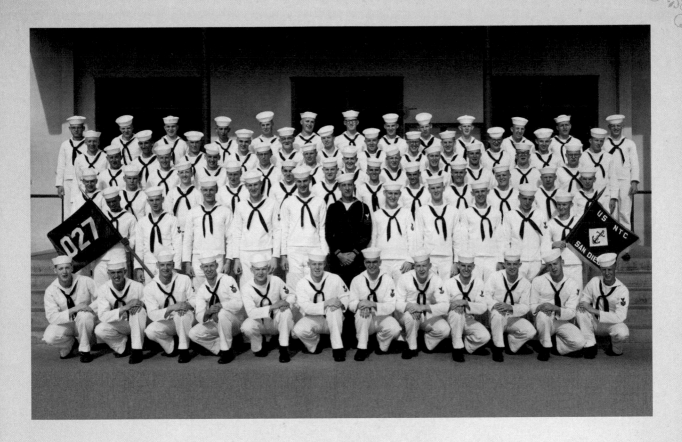

RESPONSE TOOK THE WIND OUT OF HIS SAILS

As the smallest man in the company, I was the right guide, a position that marches ahead of the tallest guys, who are in the front row. At the end of every day, we washed the clothes we'd worn. The Navy's technique for drying clothes involved a special way of tying them on a clothesline with twine. When I asked the company commander if he'd heard of clothespins, he gave me 25 pushups. I didn't ask any more questions. That's me holding the flag at far right.

JAMES JANS · BENSON, AZ

LAUNDRY CYCLE

At Officer Candidates School in 1966, a Marine Corps photographer posed me by the Potomac River. I was sliding down the muddy bank, irritated that I'd have to once again wash, iron and starch my utilities.

DAVID NELSON · HOUSTON, TX

Real-Life MASH Surgeon

Short on medical specialists as the Korean War began, the Army drafted them. One young doctor worked in the mobile hospital that inspired the famous 4077th.

DAVE HICKEY · WAUKESHA, WI

Dave's father, Dr. Hugh Hickey, took this photograph of a helicopter arriving at the 8055th. All of the photos in this story are from Dr. Hickey's personal collection.

May 16, 1951: My sister Sue is born. My dad, Hugh Hickey, was also born on that date, in 1925. The day Sue was born, Dad was 5,870 miles away from his family, serving in a Mobile Army Surgical Hospital in Korea.

In December 1950 my dad, then a surgical resident at Henry Ford Hospital in Detroit, Michigan, received his orders for active military service. Dad left his young wife, also named Sue, and his baby son—me—and went to Korea to serve in the MASH unit that was to eventually become a model for a book and, later, a movie and a TV series.

Dad's fellow Army surgeon, H. Richard Hornberger, wrote *MASH: A Novel About Three Army Doctors*, based on his experience in Korea. The book, which was published under the name Richard Hooker in 1968, is a dark comedy about operations in the hellscape of a divided land.

Dr. Hickey next to the sign designating his MASH unit in Korea, the 8055th, nicknamed "Eight Oh Double Nickel."

Dad's service in the 8055th ("Eight Oh Double Nickel") MASH unit added to the family legacy of battlefield medicine: In 1862, during the Civil War, my great-great-grandfather Charles Rodebaugh fought in the battle of Shiloh, which had the first effective, documented U.S. Army field hospitals.

Casualties of the Conflict

South Korea had been invaded twice from the north since June 1950, and, as it is for all war-ravaged countries, its living conditions were desperate. My dad told us about the Maryknoll Sisters in Seoul who selflessly cared for Korean children orphaned by the war. Sister Mary Mercy Hirschboeck, a native of Milwaukee, Wisconsin, our family home, was the first physician to enter the Maryknoll order.

She and other Maryknoll sisters established a clinic in Pusan, Korea, in 1951, during the height of the conflict. Somehow they clothed, fed, sheltered, medically treated and protected children of all ages who lived in a city that had been absolutely decimated. Dad and his fellow MASH members did what they could, when they could, to provide medical aid to these children, even though conditions in the MASH units in Korea were primitive compared to today's units.

The movie and the TV show, both called *M*A*S*H*—Hollywood added the asterisks to Hooker's title—portrayed some of the harsh conditions Dad lived and worked in, but they could not convey the bone-chilling cold of Korea's winters, nor the sweltering heat of its summers. The MASH units were near the front, and staff and

Injured soldiers were moved from helicopters, left, to medical tents. Below, Dr. Hickey holds a scalpel.

Conditions in the MASH units were primitive compared to today's units.

personnel lived in canvas tents and performed their duties outside in all imaginable weather. For the U.S. Army surgeons, the days and hours fluctuated between boredom and exhausting effort.

The operating rooms were set up inside large tents, where it was not uncommon for a lightbulb to explode over the operating table, sending shards of glass into open wounds. The medical staff pieced together the broken bodies of wounded U.S., United Nations and South Korean military personnel, and despite gallant efforts—sterile was only a word—preventing infection was a constant challenge. Often, doctors could perform only "meatball surgery," which simply stabilized the wounded soldier's condition to save his life.

Medical personnel saw every kind of trauma that the terrible weapons of war could cause,

including live rounds embedded in wounds. The MASH units' doctors, nurses and other medical staff also provided care to North Korean and Chinese soldiers; no distinction was made when it came to human life. Despite all the challenges they faced, the surgeons saved countless lives. For the wounded who made it to a MASH unit, the chance of survival was more than 97%.

As Seen on TV

Opening scenes in both the movie and TV series show helicopters bringing wounded soldiers to a MASH for treatment, an accurate portrayal of the real deal. The helicopters that U.N. forces used were lifesavers, transporting injured troops directly from the battlefield, and—when necessary—from the MASH to hospitals away from the front lines.

Dr. Hickey visits with children from the Maryknoll orphanage, right. Below, at the 38th parallel, the Demilitarized Zone dividing the Korean peninsula.

The nursing corps in the MASH units were the backbone of the medical operation.

When helicopters were inbound with casualties, Dad and others rushed to the helipads. On arrival, the wounded were moved directly to surgical tents for immediate treatment. The iconic Bell H-13 Sioux bubble-cockpit models, which had side-mounted stretcher pods, were most commonly used to transport injured troops from the front lines. After patients reached the MASH units, the Sikorsky H-19 Chickasaw helicopters could take them to hospitals farther from the front lines.

Along with his service in Korea, Dad worked in a U.S. military hospital in Japan, where the most severely wounded were transferred from Seoul in military C-47 transport planes. There, patients received the best medical and surgical care available at the time. Dad felt strongly that the surgical training he got during his military service could not have been duplicated in a civilian setting.

Camp Characters

Who was the real-life Hawkeye Pierce? For that matter, whom did Hornberger base any of his main characters on? Dad exhibited many traits of Alan Alda's version of Hawkeye: charm, wit (Dad loved limericks) and an incredible bedside manner. We liked to think that Hawkeye—and the rest of the *M*A*S*H* characters—were composites of Hornberger's fellow inmates. That is, except for the nurse character famously called Hot Lips. Yes, she existed. Dad had a picture (Page 131) he took of the nurses in his MASH unit, but he never told us whether Hot Lips was in that photograph.

The nursing corps in the MASH units were, as they always are, the backbone of the medical operation. Many of the nurses in Korea were World War II veterans who chose to serve again in a war zone. Dad always praised the nurses as excellent medical practitioners, and for their skill at boosting the morale of the patients, medical staff and personnel.

Many countries joined the U.S. in fighting in Korea, acting under the umbrella of the U.N. Among these were Britain, Canada and Turkey. Dad remembered that the Turkish soldiers

Dr. Hugh Hickey took this picture of a chopper outfitted to carry the wounded from battlefields in Korea to mobile hospitals close to the front.

Dr. Hickey captured his fellow surgeons in a lighthearted moment. Dr. Hornberger, aka *MASH* author Richard Hooker, is on the right.

especially were incredibly tough, braving their wounds with great courage. He also socialized occasionally with the Brits. Dad, like everyone there, needed relief from the constant stress of wartime service, and he told us the British officers were especially adept at stepping away from the fray. Although Dad was never much of a drinker, he related memories of off-duty evenings with the Brits. He always paid for it the next morning.

Remembering the War

Dad returned home in 1952 and began a long, successful career as an orthopedic surgeon. He and Mom went on to raise eight children, and he enjoyed a full life in the company of friends and family. But the time he spent in Korea transformed his life as only war can.

My parents attended some of the 8055th MASH reunions. Hornberger also attended the reunions, and I heard that Alan Alda attended one, too. War forges strong bonds, and those of the members of the 8055th MASH were no exception.

My wife, Pat, and I visited Korea in June 2010, the 60th anniversary of the start of the conflict. Our daughter Beth was teaching high school in Uijeongbu, near Seoul. On that trip we visited the Demilitarized Zone on the 38th parallel, as well as Panmunjom, the site of the Korean War truce talks. We could stand in North Korea, on the north side of the U.N. command's blue quonset hut.

War forges strong bonds, and those of the members of the 8055th MASH were no exception.

The South Koreans we met expressed gratitude for the sacrifices American service members made in their country during that awful time. After, we shared the pictures and stories of our adventures in Korea with Dad, who was in poor health. He died later that year, but I sensed that our account of traveling in a peaceful and prosperous South Korea brought back bittersweet memories for him.

In 2017, while in Washington, D.C., to attend my 45th reunion at Georgetown University, we visited the Korean War Veterans Memorial on the National Mall. It is a haunting commemoration of a conflict sometimes called the Forgotten War, although it is by no means forgotten by the many thousands who served there, nor by their families.

The Mural Wall at the memorial includes thousands of photographs etched into granite, and as we approached the memorial that day, I noticed a picture of a doctor in a surgical cap and mask. I like to think it's my father, a fitting tribute to him and all medical personnel who served and gave so much in Korea.

Dr. Hornberger stands atop a partly submerged tank.

THE MAN BEHIND *M*A*S*H*

Dr. H. Richard Hornberger's story of treating war's casualties, told with razor-sharp humor, brought a cast of iconic characters to life.

Like many recent medical school graduates in the early 1950s, Hornberger was sent to Korea to serve as a U.S. Army surgeon. Wartime experience was hard to shake, and when Hornberger returned, he began to write about his surgical exploits during the war, treating the subject with gallows humor. He worked on the story with sportswriter and war correspondent W.C. Heinz, and found a publisher for *MASH: A Novel About Three Army Doctors* in 1968.

....

In 1970, Robert Altman directed a movie based on the book about the fictional 4077th. The success of the movie, the third-highest-grossing film that year, led to a series on CBS. The Korean War lasted a little more than three years, but the popular series ran for more than three times that long, from 1972 until 1983.

....

According to his son William, Hornberger wrote the book as a humorous account, and never intended it to have an antiwar message. William claimed that Capt. Benjamin Franklin (Hawkeye) Pierce was based on Dr. Hornberger, who ultimately disliked Alan Alda's TV portrayal of the war-weary doctor.

NATALIE WYSONG

Childhood friends Harry, left, and Philip learned they were stationed close to each other during the Korean War.

Friends Find Each Other in Korea

Michigan classmates served together.

Philip Allen and I grew up in houses about 50 yards apart in Birmingham, Michigan. We stayed friends throughout childhood and high school, then we attended Michigan State College (now University) together. We joined different branches of the service and we each reached the rank of lieutenant.

In Korea, Philip served with the 67th Tactical Reconnaissance Wing of the Air Force, and I went to the front line with the Army's 7th Division, 73rd Tank Battalion. After exchanging a couple of letters, we realized that we were stationed within about 40 miles of each other, so in spring 1953 we arranged for Philip to visit me at my base, northeast of his location.

It proved to be a more complicated journey than we'd thought because Philip had to skirt the mountains to reach me. He first drove south through Seoul, then north to the Army base. I took Philip on a tour of battle sites, including Pork

Chop Hill. He later told our hometown newspaper, *The Birmingham Eccentric*, which reported on our meeting in Korea, that the tour gave him a better appreciation for the ground fight and a vivid understanding of the war.

Philip and I met in Seoul a few times after that before we returned home. We were in each other's wedding parties and got together frequently before he moved to California.

Philip died a few years ago, and I have reached my ninth decade (and I am doing well for my vintage). But I have an enduring memory of when we were kids together, building soapbox racers with other boys out of whatever we could find— ironing boards, orange crates. All was well until we all got mad at each other and each boy would take back his contribution. That would last a couple of days before we'd get together again to start a different project.

HARRY WAGNER · WHITE LAKE, MI

Rough Takeoff

As Air Force geared up, new recruits felt the crunch.

Early in January 1951, this newly enlisted 20-year-old with dreams of learning to fly boarded a bus in Kalamazoo and then a train in Detroit. The early 1950s were a period of buildup for the Air Force, a relatively new branch of the military that was adjusting to the requirements for the Korean War. The train was filled with hundreds of other recruits just like me, on our way to basic military training at Lackland Air Force Base in San Antonio, Texas.

During the three-day journey, our train stopped frequently to give freight trains the right of way. We finally arrived at a field dotted with dozens of open-air canopies, each big enough for six recruits. Each shelter had a bucket of water and towel. Nearby were woods. At mealtimes, we were led to a mess hall after the enlisted men were finished eating; the rest of the time we sat on the ground. When darkness fell, we shivered on the bare ground under the canopy without beds or blankets.

The next morning, I spied cardboard in the parking lot behind the PX. We planned to bring it to our shelter, but base security spotted us and ordered us back. We tried again the following day, and this time, we evaded security, and got the cardboard: Our third night was tolerable.

The next day, we boarded military buses. As we left the base, we noticed trucks arriving and saw workmen unloading cots and bedding at the shelters. We breathed a sigh of relief. When we returned to the field later, our hearts sank: The shelters now contained six cots apiece, but the bedding was gone. In the week that followed, we were issued pants and dog tags, but we still wore the shirts we had on when we left home.

After 11 days in that Texas field, we were processed and dispatched to various Air Force bases. I transferred to Lowry Air Force Base in Denver, Colorado. There I saw a newspaper, which reported that officials in Washington, D.C., had ordered an inspection at Lackland after hearing about an influx of recruits dispatched to an empty field without gear or supplies.

Lackland officials had hastily arranged for supplies to be brought to camp to satisfy inspectors. After they left, bedding was returned to wherever it came from, probably the airmen in the barracks.

I'm grateful I survived the ordeal without getting sick, and I learned that perspective is everything. Although Colorado was colder than Texas, sleeping in coal-fired, heated barracks was very comfortable.

NORMAN "BUD" PEACOCK
BLISSFIELD, MI

Bud, in his uniform, next to wife, Joann, along with brother Don and Don's wife, Catherine, in Alamo, MI, in 1952.

Candidate Super Surfer

Leaders in training gave buddy a lift.

Some college pals and I enrolled in platoon leader class in the summer of 1967, and were sent to boot camp at Marine Corps Base Quantico in Virginia. I was soon engaged in previously unimagined activities at Camp Upshur (not so fondly remembered as "Camp Rupture").

Moments after our arrival, the drill instructor ordered all 50 of us to crowd through a hatchlike entrance into a Quonset hut, where we dumped the contents of our suitcases on our "racks" (the beds). The instructor confiscated contraband—colorful pajamas, aftershave—and used it for entertainment as we stood at attention.

I'd brought with me a wonderfully executed black-and-white photo that a girlfriend had taken. It was a desert tortoise, its tracks diminishing into a distant New Mexico sand dune. The instructor's nose was pretty close to mine as he screamed "What IS this, Candidate?"

I don't know what prompted my response, but I yelled back "Platoon Sergeant, that is Candidate Super Surfer!" Without a pause, he asked me why Candidate Super Surfer was not present, and ordered him to join our group immediately.

My dilemma gave me nightmares, and I wrote the girlfriend who'd taken the picture, pleading for help. In the meantime, my sergeant apparently forgot about it. About a month later, I got an order to report to the company office, a place we never wanted to go.

Inside, I found company officers inspecting a shoebox covered with small holes. I heard scratching; the package moved. Candidate Super Surfer had arrived. I lamely reminded the officers that the animal had been ordered to join us, and then prepared to hit the deck for pushups. Instead, the sergeant assigned several duties regarding the new arrival.

I was to ensure it had a comfortable rack for taps at night, to feed it properly (heisting food from the mess was taboo), to take it everywhere the platoon went and to make sure it could pass the final physical fitness test.

Getting the extra slice of tomato or leaf of lettuce was easier than winning the support of my platoon mates. We took turns carrying the heavy metal ammo can with Candidate Super Surfer in it on our daily runs, forced marches, close-order drills and field problems in the humid heat.

Candidate Super Surfer and I passed our qualifying exams, and were ready to go on to other things. We held an informal ceremony and released him into the forest.

STEVE SCARANO • VISTA, CA

Candidate Scarano, back right, ready to compete in a physical-readiness test. Candidate Super Surfer is not present.

ROLL CALL

Donald can't recall all names, but knows Billie Williams, "Rat" Edwarsa, Billi Tucker, Paul Malone and John Bapcock.

TORPEDO SQUADRON 20

When a hurricane was expected to hit our Naval air station at Edenton, North Carolina, in September 1945, we evacuated to this Army hospital in Martinsburg, West Virginia. We stayed in an empty ward of the hospital's mental wing. I took this picture of my fellow members of Torpedo Squadron 20 on the steps leading out of the ward.

DONALD NAGLE · LEROY, NY

SALT AND SNAKES

I served in the 263rd Medical Battalion, 3rd Amphibious Brigade, from 1943-'46. Some of my happiest memories are of my Army buddies and their antics.

I once was served apple pie with salt—someone used salt instead of sugar in the recipe, either by mistake or by design.

I still have a photograph of a bunch of them holding up a 10-foot-long snake we caught one afternoon.

If these incidents stir up any memories, please write to me. I'd love to hear from you.

SALVATORE FANTASIA · ANTELOPE, CA

Salvatore has fond memories of kidding around with his Army buddies.

Meeting Brother Grub

Training mascot doled out the pushups.

Artillery school at Fort Sill, Oklahoma, in 1975 was divided into training for towed and self-propelled howitzers. I was assigned to the self-propelled group, but during our tour, we were required to do a week of cross-training on the other artillery type.

During the class on the towed artillery, the sergeant asked us questions out of the blue. He pointed at a hapless student: "Private! What is the main difference between the screw breech of this artillery piece and a standard screw breech?"

If the student answered correctly that the breech was two-stage, rather than one, he was allowed to stay seated. If he couldn't answer, the student assumed what was known as the "front leaning rest" position—a pushup—over a crack in the concrete.

The crack was supposedly inhabited by Brother Grub, and after the student apologized for his incorrect answer, the sergeant asked what Brother Grub's response was. The student would reply, "Brother Grub says to do 20 pushups!" and perform the exercise.

Midway through one cross-training, Private Pierre failed to answer a question. He dutifully assumed the front leaning rest over Brother Grub.

Almost immediately, he started to laugh.

"Why are you laughing, Private?" the sergeant demanded.

Looking into the crack in the concrete, Pierre said, "Brother Grub ain't nothin' but a peanut!"

Fighting back a smile, the instructor ordered Pierre to apologize to Brother Grub for calling him a peanut, which Pierre did.

The sergeant asked him what Brother Grub's answer was, meaning it was time for the soldier to do pushups.

Without hesitation, Pierre answered, "Brother Grub says I'm one cool dude, and should sit back down."

Everybody burst into laughter. Pierre was allowed to sit down without doing any pushups, but we were instructed that there would be no more "cool dudes" in the class.

I enjoyed imagining how Brother Grub came into being: After a duty day, the sergeants sat around the artillery piece having a beer, eating peanuts and relaxing as they reviewed the day's training. One of them dropped a peanut that rolled into the crack in the concrete floor, and Brother Grub was born.

RON PONIATOWSKI · BARABOO, WI

Detachment Cartoonist

Drill instructor had another dimension.

A fter saying my goodbyes in Detroit in February 1957, I boarded a plane bound for Lackland Air Force Base in San Antonio, Texas. I had six weeks of basic training before I would be sent to air traffic control school at Keesler Air Force Base in Biloxi, Mississippi.

The training was physically and mentally demanding, and recruits all tried to avoid getting extra duties such as scrubbing the barracks floor with a toothbrush—which I had to do—or cleaning the 10 latrines.

During rare moments of downtime, I liked to sketch. In high school I'd gotten good at drawing cartoons and caricatures of the people I observed. At the end of one exhausting day of exercises and drills, I was relaxing in the barracks. I was making a sketch of one of our drill instructors, barking orders and calling all of us unmentionable names.

The other recruits gathered around and were laughing at my cartoon when the drill instructor walked in and demanded to know what the ruckus was about.

Fearing for my life—or at least the fate of cleaning latrines for a week—I showed him the caricature.

Silence.

"Is that supposed to be me?" he asked.

Then, to my amazement, he laughed, and asked if he could have the drawing.

After that, word of my sketches got around, and soon the other drill instructors were excusing me from daily regimens so I could fulfill their drawing requests. In fact, an hour before I graduated as an airman third class, I was putting the finishing touches on my final caricature!

I gave away all of the drawings I made in boot camp—it would sure be fun to see one of them now.

JAMES FARKAS · NORTHVILLE, MI   James' pastime drew attention in the barracks.

Pointless Sewing Project

New Airmen lost their stripes.

After high school in Yeadon, Pennsylvania, I dreamed of becoming a horse farrier, but went with my second, more realistic, choice—the Air Force.

I embraced basic training at Lackland Air Force Base in San Antonio, Texas, and I tried for perfection in learning the regulations and performing the many drills in boot camp. After finally earning our airman stripes, our squadron had prepared for a presentation in front of the base commander to showcase our achievement. Our training instructor, Tech. Sgt. Snapper, was pleased with the precision of our marching drill and gave us a rare afternoon off. The only catch was that one of us had to sew the new chevrons onto the squad's uniform blouses. I drew the short stick.

I could shoe a horse, sling bales of hay and put up fence, but sewing wasn't for me. My new task quickly became a home economics nightmare: On my first attempt, I sewed the stripe and the blouse sleeve to my pants. On the second try, I sewed the sleeve shut. Pressed for time, I had to resort to gluing the stripes onto our dress blue blouses.

As we lined up in the Texas heat the next day, my squad mates expressed admiration for my "sewing." At the words "Parade, rest!" we shared smiles for a great job representing our squad.

But a moment later, I heard: "Airman Cristofaro, front and center. On the double."

I approached Tech. Sgt. Snapper, who turned me to face the class. The tarmac around my flight mates was littered with fallen stripes, curled from the glue that had melted in the 101-degree heat.

I wondered how many KP assignments and nights of dorm guard I had coming.

Then I saw the hint of a smile.

We were called to stand at attention as the base commander marched over and

Kathleen was very proud to have earned her airman's stripes.

demanded to know which bozo was responsible for the mess. I stood at attention and loudly said, "I am the bozo, sir. Please accept my apology."

A look passed between the commander and Tech. Sgt. Snapper before they both doubled over in laughter.

Instead of being reprimanded, I had to pick up all of the stripes littering the tarmac. And after we marched back to the barracks, one of the gals in my dorm offered to help me sew the stripes on, for real this time.

KATHLEEN DOLL CRISTOFARO
ALDAN, PA

Peacetime Sightseeing

I was part of forces stationed in Japan after
World War II. Here I enjoyed a rickshaw tour of Kobe.

MALCOLM FIFE · FOUNTAIN RUN, KY

CHAPTER 7

MOTORING MEMORIES

From putting a new romance into drive
to summoning happy memories from
years past, there's nothing quite
like a vintage ride.

Working Goats

Four-wheeled carriages filled with young passengers meant hefty loads
for the goats at New York's Coney Island in 1904.

Glenn in one of the grand courts on the grounds of the world's fair.

Honeymoon Out West

Railroad job let newlyweds explore California.

Bess at the Palace of Horticulture, left, and in front of the Tower of Jewels, above.

*One of the places the newlyweds most enjoyed
visiting was the world's fair.*

My grandmother Bess made sure my clothes—and our house—were clean, she made my lunch when I came home from Northwood Elementary and she let me watch a 15-minute segment of her soap opera before I returned to school. She was a mother figure for most of my childhood, and I concluded that she'd always lived right there, in Columbus, Ohio.

That is, until I came across a picture of Bess looking as if she'd come right out of the pages of *Vogue*. My questions about that photo led me to discover the existence of a whole new chapter in my grandparents' lives.

Bess met my grandfather Glenn at a party in Cleveland when he was home visiting his parents. Glenn, a civil engineer, worked for the Central Pacific Railroad in California. After a period of correspondence between them, Bess took the train from Columbus to Ogden, Utah, where they were married on Feb. 13, 1915. The couple lived in Sacramento while Glenn finished his contract with the railroad.

In 1915, California—and much of the country—was abuzz with excitement about the Panama-Pacific International Exposition. This event was planned to celebrate the completion of the Panama Canal and the rise of the U.S. to the world stage. All of San Francisco was eager to show that it had recovered from the horrific 1906 earthquake, and thought of the event simply as its world's fair.

Because of Glenn's work with Central Pacific, the young couple were able to travel by train to many sites in California. One of the places the newlyweds most enjoyed visiting was the world's fair, to which they returned several times.

My grandparents referred to the months they lived out west as their honeymoon. Memories of that time were precious, especially later when Glenn lost his job, as well as the family farm, and they suffered other indignities of the Great Depression. I'm very grateful that I have these glamorous photos of my Ohio grandparents and their 1915 honeymoon.

MARTY COTTRILL · CENTERVILLE, OH

Ron, in striped shirt, posed on the vintage tank with friends Randy LaRue and Rodney Ziolkowski.

First Crush Is 16-Ton Heartbreaker

He kept Charlie's tank in his sights.

Model rockets, planes and ships filled the shelves in my room in 1967. The most fascinating of all to me were tanks.

On the back roads of the route from Racine, Wisconsin, to my grandparents' house, I saw a tank with "for sale" painted on its army-green side. With big white stars on its turret and nose, the vintage M3A3 Stuart tank was a fearsome beast. I begged Dad to stop. Its owner, Charlie, said that it cost much more than the $20 I had.

Dad allowed me to climb on the tank only once, but I saw it every time we drove past.

"Dad, the tank's still there," I hinted. "Maybe I can play on it again."

"Maybe," he said, which meant no.

I needed an angle.

The campaign continued when my friend Rodney was over. "Rodney's dad drove Sherman tanks, and Rodney's never seen a real tank. Maybe we could take him to see Charlie's tank on Saturday!"

The boys inspected the tank, even though, Ron says, "None of us had any idea what we were looking at."

Maybe this time, I'd be able to park that tracked beauty in my own backyard.

"If the weather's good," Dad said, which he thought gave him a fighting chance.

Saturday's weather was perfect for a trip to climb on a steel mountain. With a little more urging, Dad set out with me and my friends Rodney and Randy, who wore his Sunday best. Some boys, including Charlie's son, were already there playing army. Finally I got up the nerve to ask them if we could go inside the tank. Before we climbed in, Dad said, "Don't touch anything!"

Dropping through the driver's hatch, I gawked at the controls and wires. We explored honeycombed ammo racks and a floor hanging from the turret ring. It was a dream come true.

One day, the tank was gone. Its disappearance put me in a gloomy mood for a long time.

I found out from Charlie that he'd sold the tank and bought a ski hill with the proceeds, but he told us where the new owner lived. Dad wasn't happy to learn this, because it meant another trip out into the country. I was thrilled that I might see the tank again, and maybe this time I'd be able to park that

tracked beauty in my own backyard. I'd worry about how to pay for it later.

A few weeks later, we took the long drive. There, hidden under a tarp, was Charlie's tank. To my disappointment, the owner had a new buyer—he was selling it to a police department. The sum was still much more than I had. I slunk back to the car.

Charlie's tank was gone, but not my love of tanking. In the military, I crewed self-propelled howitzers. As a civilian, I drove vintage tanks for collectors and museums. I know all about old tanks, but whenever I hear about one for sale, it's always a case of being a day late or more than a dollar short.

My wife assures me that I'm fine without owning a tank, because she loves me all the same (she's always been a bit odd that way).

But I can't help thinking about the empty spot near the house, which would look good with an old Stuart like Charlie's tank.

RON PONIATOWSKI · BARABOO, WI

GOAT CARTS

GIDDYUP, BABY ⌃
My mother, Elizabeth, kept all of the family photos from her parents, Herman and Flora Baxter. In this 1928 photo, their children, standing from left, are June, Elizabeth, Marjorie and Cleo. Herman Jr., got to sit in the cart.
DAVID M. HABBEN ·
BOISE, ID

TAKE THE REINS »
It took a sturdy goat to pull this wagon with three children in Eden Park in Cincinnati, Ohio, in 1906. This image is from the Library of Congress.

GOAT-RABBIT ⌃
Terrence Gene, my little brother, was 2 and I was 6 in 1936 when we sat for this picture in Great Falls, Montana.
ED WEBER • KEIZER, OR

SITTING PRETTY »
This picture of my grandmother Catherine Nichols and her brother Raymond was taken in Louisville in the year 1924, when she was 4.
KAREN HAMILTON
COXS CREEK, KY

It's a Bug's Life

Buzzing around in the Beetle.

———

My mother, Lois, chipped in half the money when I bought a Volkswagen Beetle from a boy down the street. I'd learned to drive in Mom's Chevy, which had automatic transmission, and mastering the VW's manual transmission was a challenge.

On level surfaces I did pretty well. But on our Los Angeles hills I panicked, especially if I rolled backward when a car was behind me. With my boyfriend, David, I practiced braking and starting. I was proud when I mastered using the clutch and accelerator in perfect harmony, and I felt competent to drive anywhere—until my friend Nancy and I went to San Francisco.

Those hills were terrifying. We parked in an angled stall to have lunch at a Chinese restaurant.

The car almost tipped sideways, and when we left, it wouldn't start. The restaurant employees helped us push the car upright to get it going.

After David and I married, he started working in downtown Los Angeles. One day he drove my Bug to work, and the car was stolen. I was heartbroken until it was recovered. Luckily it returned to me mostly undamaged—except for the starter, which needed to be replaced because the car had been hot-wired.

I drove that VW Beetle for many more years, but I wound up giving it up when our second child was born. I loved that car almost as much as I loved my sweetheart!

SHELLY SHARP · YORBA LINDA, CA

Shelly and David get ready for her senior prom in 1970.

"The blue car" was passed through the family with the promise of eternal ownership.

True Blue to Camaro

Family honors preservation pledge.

———

Automobiles, and the love of them, are part of my DNA. My parents drove amazing cars—Chevelle, Skylark, Corvette, Riviera— equipped with the most powerful engines available—396, 401, 454, 455. My mom, Dodie Stuhr, aces all the "Name That Car" quizzes.

Her 1967 Chevrolet Camaro RS is typically pegged for the wrong year. That car was sold new at Lindekugel Chevrolet and has spent its entire life roaming the streets of Owatonna, Minnesota.

Mom's sister, Deanne, was the Camaro's second owner, trading in her Corvair for it in 1970, for the used-car price of $1,795. After Deanne died, my grandparents Elmer and Gladys Stuhr kept the car

for a year, and then it came to Mom, with one condition: She had to keep it forever!

We used the "blue car," as my nephew named it, as a daily driver until Minnesota winters took a toll. The car underwent a full restoration: A local shop did the bodywork and painted it; my dad replaced and restored the interior. Now the Camaro is stored during the wintertime.

The car is fun to drive, but it has no power steering or power brakes, and for air conditioning, you adjust the vent windows and keep moving!

After 50 years (and-counting) of ownership, I think my grandparents would be pleased.

SHANE DANIELSON · ROCHESTER, MN

Richard stands next to the family car in 1952. "I guess I did look a little young!"

Short Drive, Shorter Driver

Pulled over for a height violation.

▬▬▬

After passing both the written and road tests in the summer of 1952, at the age of 16, I was issued my temporary driver's permit for the state of Massachusetts.

The next Sunday, I persuaded my father to allow me to drive on an afternoon visit to my grandparents in the town of Ware, Massachusetts, off Route 9, about 25 miles west of our home in Worcester.

Thrilled at the opportunity, I got behind the wheel, with my father in the passenger seat and my mother in the back.

About halfway there, with a glance in the rearview mirror, I saw a state police cruiser, blue lights flashing, following us. I told my father, who very calmly instructed me to pull onto the shoulder of the road.

The state trooper, imposing in his crisp blue uniform and highly polished boots, approached.

The trooper reassured me that I wasn't doing anything wrong. However, he said that I looked a little young to be driving. He asked if I had a driver's license.

I proudly pulled out my recently issued permit. Somewhat surprised that I had one, the trooper suggested that the next time I drive, I should sit on a pillow.

"But officer," I replied. "I am sitting on one!"

He chuckled and returned my permit with a caution to drive carefully, and walked back to his cruiser.

That experience, while it happened long ago, is still is a pleasant memory today.

RICHARD RENIERE · HAMPTON, NH

Couple's First Scrape

Drive-in date survives a little ding.

June 1959 found me at National Guard camp in Helena, Montana. After hours, I was cruising with two of my classmates from high school, also members of the National Guard, when we passed a car with three girls in it. Stories vary as to who honked at whom, but in any case, we all stopped and introductions ensued. We arranged dates for the next night—mine was Norma Jo Riley.

Norma's mother allowed us to borrow her new car—a '59 Ford Fairlane—for our date to the drive-in movie. I was in heaven, driving a beautiful tan and white car with a beautiful date.

When the movie was over, I thought Norma should have a chance to drive her mother's new car. Norma informed me she couldn't drive, but as a teenager who loved cars and driving I just couldn't comprehend that anyone my age wouldn't know how to drive. So I convinced her to get behind the wheel. I immediately realized I'd made a mistake: As Norma pulled out of our parking space, she made a sharp turn, hitting the speaker post with the rear door and, unfortunately, damaging the beautiful new car that had been trusted to my care just hours before.

That's it, I thought. I won't be seeing this girl again.

To our amazement, we were pardoned. Norma and I went out every night that I had free before our unit returned to Kalispell. After that, we stayed in touch while I worked construction that summer on the new Air Force base in Glasgow and when I went back to college. Sometime during the year of this steady relationship, our talk turned to marriage.

Norma's mother was all for the marriage. My future father-in-law, Norman, a gentle soul and a smart man, stayed out of the way of the wedding plans. We married Dec. 10, 1960, but the day itself is a blur. I do

After much preparation, Norma and William's wedding day in 1960 went by too quickly.

remember it as one of the few times in my life when my mom, my dad and I were together, since my parents had divorced when I was 3.

Now in the winter of my life, I can truly say one of life's greatest gifts is being able to love and support one another, and I understand how lucky I was that the horn honked so many years ago.

WILLIAM GLASS · FEDERAL WAY, WA

Chuck and Bill dig in to their campfire meal.

Downright Excitin' Ranch Vacation

Chicago greenhorns rode the iron horse out west.

When I was 5, my parents wanted to give me and my 7-year-old brother, Chuck, a taste of western culture.

In preparation, they sent us in 1952 to riding school at Doyle's Stables in Wheeling, Illinois, for a few months of Horsemanship 101. We lived in the beautiful neighboring western suburb of River Forest. Our mom, Dorothy, was a homemaker, but she had worked for the Chicago Great Western Railway on Michigan Avenue until she married our dad, Wil, in 1941. Dad was vice president of The Rockwood Co., an insurance and bond brokerage in the Chicago loop.

That summer, our family boarded the Denver Zephyr for a train ride west, bound for Rocky Mountain adventures at the rustic S-Bar-V dude ranch near Winter Park, Colorado. Chuck and I were straight out of suburban Chicago, with our brand-spanking-new cowboy shirts and stiff dungarees, probably purchased by Mom at Marshall Field's.

During our two-week stay at the S-Bar-V, we went on trail rides, ate our meals family-style in the dining room, sang around many campfires and attended local rodeos. The grownups had happy hour cocktails with similarly minded guests (even though alcohol was prohibited at the ranch).

Mom asked the ranch hand to assign her the oldest, slowest and laziest nag on hand for the trail rides. Queenie got the assignment, and Mom never fell off, despite not having the riding lessons that Chuck and I got.

When we got home, I brought new energy to our neighborhood games of cowboys and Indians. Mom and Dad never let me buy my own cap gun, much less the coveted Red Ryder BB gun.

We never went back to the S-Bar-V, although in later years when my wife and I took the train west, I saw the former site of the ranch as we came through the Moffat Tunnel.

It is now called Winter Park Resort and all of the iconic and rustic ranch buildings are gone.

The trip to the S-Bar-V on the Denver Zephyr was a beautiful, unforgettable trip.

BILL KUHLMAN · TUCSON, AZ

Top: Cowboy Sandy shows the city slickers how to handle a lariat. Bottom left: The boys are ready to saddle up, while Mom gets to know Queenie. Bottom right: Bill learns the ropes with Sandy's help.

The trip to the S-Bar-V on the Denver Zephyr was a beautiful, unforgettable trip.

ON THE ROAD

New models and improved technologies promised travelers an exciting (and most importantly, breakdown-free) trip.

Pinto Wagon is the basic wagon idea all over again: lots of space for little money.

1973 »

Back to Basics

The oil crisis of the 1970s forced carmakers to shorten their wagons for fuel economy. The compact Pinto wagon became synonymous with "cheap" family vehicle. Pinto was known as "the car nobody loved, but everybody bought." Ford sold more than 2 million of them.

When Ford pioneered the station wagon in 1929, we simply combined a durable, economical car with a lot of space in back.

That's exactly what we've done with the Pinto Wagon. We've taken the durable, economical Pinto—and given it over 60 cubic feet of cargo space. (Vega Kammback and VW Squareback give you about 50.) The rear seat folds down, the lift gate swings up out of the way, the spare tire is stored under the floor to maximize cargo space.

Under the hood, you'll find a 2000cc overhead cam engine as standard equipment. Also a fully synchronized 4-speed transmission. (You can opt for automatic, of course.) Plus extra strength universal and ball joints, starter motor, rear wheel bearings.

Front disc brakes are standard on Pinto Wagon. Along with rack-and-pinion steering, a body that's welded into one solid piece of steel, and a rear suspension specially designed for load-carrying.

In short, the Pinto Wagon is ideal for people who want a basic economy car that carries more—or a wagon that costs less.

Shown here is the Pinto Wagon with Squire Option, optional whitewall tires, luggage rack, deluxe bumper group, automatic transmission.

Pinto Wagons for '73, at your Ford Dealer's. Better idea for safety...buckle up!

When you get back to basics, you get back to Ford.

FORD PINTO

FORD DIVISION Ford

The Nomad—4-door 6-passenger—one of five new Chevy wagons!

« 1959

The Chevy Family

Chevrolet offered five wagon models for 1959, ranging from the entry-level two-door Brookwood (shown in red) to the top-of-the-line Nomad (top), which sold for $3,000 fully loaded. (Average annual income that year was around $5,000). The Kingswood (bottom) was massive, with a rear-facing third seat, power back window and room for nine.

THE CAR THAT LEADS YOUR KIND OF LIFE-'59 CHEVROLET!

Just look at the practical way the '59 Chevy meets the needs of today's on-the-go family. Its famous Body by Fisher is roomier, with vast new areas of visibility. Its ride is smoother, handling is easier. Its finish keeps its shine for as long as three years without wax or polish. There's a peppery new 6 that gets up to 10% more miles per gallon—plus a whole lineup of vim-packed V8's.

And look at the beautiful variety of versatile Chevrolet station wagons for '59. All five models offer the last word in station wagon practicality. Handy around the homestead. Great for trips. Some day soon, take the whole family along to see the '59 Chevy— the car that's shaped to the new American taste! . . . Chevrolet Division of General Motors, Detroit 2, Michigan.

The Brookwood—2-door 6-passenger. Also a 4-door Brookwood.

CHEVROLET

What America wants, America gets in a Chevy!

The Parkwood—4-door 6-passenger.

The Kingswood—4-door 9-passenger with new rear-facing third seat.

BUILT BY *Firestone*

THREE years ago Firestone established its own factories for the manufacture of batteries, spark plugs and brake linings to give owners of automobiles, trucks and buses the extra quality and service in these important automotive products that Firestone builds into its tires.

Firestone engineers and chemists developed a new porous rubber separator for Firestone EXTRA POWER batteries which allows the full sized, pure antimony lead plates not only to operate more efficiently—give extra power and quicker starting, but also give longer life.

In the manufacture of spark plugs Firestone Steel Plant Metallurgists developed and perfected new center electrodes of very fine texture which provide greater resistance to disintegration. These new electrodes assure hotter spark, more power and greatly increased life.

Firestone chemists and brake engineers found the way to make brake lining waterproof. This has been accomplished by the Firestone AQUAPRUF process whereby every asbestos fiber is saturated and coated with a special compound that gives positive braking control and freedom from chatter and squeal.

The Firestone Service Dealer or Service Store in your community will inspect your tires and test your battery, spark plugs and brakes without charge. See him today and get these better services and greater values.

Listen to Lawrence Tibbett or Richard Crooks and Harvey Firestone, Jr., every Monday night— N. B. C. Network

©1934, F. T. & R. Co.

1934 | **Building a Better Battery**

Firestone's text-heavy 1934 ad promised consumers they'd get more life out of their car's battery if they used all the company's latest innovations, including a porous rubber separator, electrodes that promised increased power and life, and waterproof brake lining. Drivers could go to their Firestone Service Dealer for an inspection "without charge."

Ray's Uncle Ed fills up as his brother, Billy, checks out Ed's Ford coupe in 1946 in Bonsack, VA.

They've Been Everywhere

Love of travel was trainman's legacy.

My grandfather Samuel T. Baldwin was born in 1880 in Bonsack, Virginia. He worked as a yard conductor for the Norfolk and Western Railway Co., a position that gave him and his family travel privileges. He and my grandmother Mattie Davis Baldwin traveled by train to the first Jamestown Exposition in Norfolk in 1907. They also went to a national convention in Washington, D.C., and in 1933 they took my mother, Edith, to the world's fair in Chicago.

My family has never been content to sit still. My mother learned to drive a Ford Model T when she was 15. My father, John, had resolved to drive one as well. He was only 12, and he and a friend wound up driving the car together, pushing pedals and steering. My parents were married in 1936, and although my mother gave up driving for a while, she took it up again when my father was drafted into the Army Air Corps during World War II.

In 1940, my parents took a lengthy trip, driving a 1938 Ford sedan from Maryland to Utah—and beyond—to visit my father's family. They made the trip with me, age 3, my Grandmother Mattie and my great-aunt Annie Davis. The 35-day trip covered 8,000 miles. We stopped at many sites, including Boulder Dam (officially Hoover Dam), the Grand Canyon and two world's fairs—in New York and San Francisco.

The travel bug has definitely spread to me and my wife, Carol. We've visited all 50 states and five Canadian provinces. As a member of the Extra Miler Club, I've visited more than 3,000 counties, boroughs and parishes in North America. Now another generation is involved in the family activity: My grandson Sage and I got to fly in a B-29, just like those my father trained in during World War II.

JOHN "RAY" FRANK · NEW MARKET, MD

Top: Ray takes a Cushman motor scooter for a test drive in 1946. Bottom left: Ray's little sister Ellen takes the pedal car for a spin in 1945. Bottom right: Ray's father, gives Black Beauty, his 10-year-old Chevy, some much-needed repair in 1946.

My family has never been content to sit still.

Texas Native Sticks Close to Home

Flattop rolled off the line when restorer graduated.

N eeding something to do when I retired in 1999, I was inspired by a friend's hobby—restoring classic cars. In 2008, I finally found the right project.

The 1959 Buick Electra was still with its original owner and had 74,000 miles on it. Parked in an open garage for 34 years, it was covered in a layer of dust and had four flat tires, a dented rear door and a cracked side window. There was no ignition key to be found. On the plus side, Blue, as I called the car, had only a little surface rust.

It also had power seats, windows, brakes and steering, along with a power antenna and a Wonder Bar radio. Under the hood was a 401-cubic-inch V-8 and automatic transmission.

By mid-2009, Blue was back in showroom condition. I've entered it in many parades and car shows, and I've brought home numerous trophies and awards.

I learned that the car was built in Arlington, Texas, and sold new from a dealership near there. It eventually was retired to the garage where I found it near Floresville—you could consider it a Texas native.

Blue's model year, 1959, is the same year I graduated from high school. It was the last year of the big fins. Car buffs call this four-door hardtop style a flattop—just like the hairstyle I wore back in high school.

MELVIN SIEBOLD · FLORESVILLE, TX

Melvin's retirement restoration project, "Blue," has seen many parades and car shows.

Arthur lost the farm car, but he gained this new beauty.

Replacement for Farm Car

Buddy sold the original.

Larry Kempkin, our car dealer in Twin Lakes, Wisconsin, sold me a 1942 Plymouth Special De Luxe in 1951 to add to my small fleet of vehicles. I liked the car except on damp days, when it carried the aroma of the farm that it came from.

Beverly and I met in 1952, and together we put a lot of miles on the farm car. Shortly after we married in 1954, I was drafted into the Army.

I sold all my cars except a 1949 Oldsmobile 88 that I saved for Beverly. The farm car went to a buddy, with the agreement that I could buy it back when I came home from the service. Upon my return in 1956, though, the car was nowhere to be seen. My buddy had found himself short of cash and sold it.

Years later, in 1987, a fellow factory worker showed me an ad from an Illinois newspaper offering a 1942 Plymouth Special De Luxe for sale. I was happy to purchase it, in this condition, for $2,000.

Back in the day, I liked to customize my vehicles, but this car—bone stock except for the custom paint job—needed nothing more. When the weather gets hot, I mount an old-time swamp cooler on the side window, but usually the cowl vent keeps us comfortable.

Beverly and I have received trophies and awards in car shows and parades, and we're looking for years of fun to come.

ARTHUR KOEHN · ARKDALE, WI

Mike was glad to find this "butternut yellow beauty," which reminds him of a car from his high school days.

Driving Passion

This love affair began in high school.

Ever since my parents brought me home from the hospital in the family's '46 Buick Roadmaster in 1951, I've been a car guy. I started going to car shows and swap meets in the '60s. The old rock 'n' roll, the like-minded people—and, of course, the cars and the many old friends I see—make the shows high points of the year for me.

I had a car just like the one pictured above when I graduated from high school in 1969. My wife-to-be, Becky, and I dated in that high school car, and after we married and had kids, it continued to serve us well into the 1980s. Rust finally put an end to it.

In 2003, I spotted an ad for this butternut yellow beauty: a 1966 Buick Skylark Gran Sport. It only needed a few slight repairs and updates, and its performance on the drive home after I bought it assured me I'd made the right choice. It's a great car for shows and cruising. My grandsons always enjoy a ride in PaPaw's hot rod, as they call it.

My favorite cars, particularly this make, are from the era I grew up in. I have another project underway to restore one as a nearly exact tribute to my high school car—it's the same color both inside and out, but the brakes and drivetrain are getting major upgrades.

Now married to me for more than 51 years, Becky still puts up with my love of all things automotive.

MIKE CARTER · NEW PLYMOUTH, OH

A Well-Tended Rose

Color combo appeals to younger generation.

This lovely coupe was the object of my admiration for years—I only wished I could afford one. I even picked out the color combination: rose mist metallic with a burgundy landau roof.

As my Ford Taurus began giving me problems, Charlie, a friend who had no family of his own, died and left his estate to us. Charlie's generosity meant I could finally afford the car of my dreams: a 1995 Mercury Cougar Bostonian Edition.

My late husband had always preferred four-door cars, but I wanted a sportier, more stylish model. I went to three dealerships looking for the exact car and color, but nothing like it was on their lots. Finally, I ordered the car just as I had imagined it.

My daughter Jeri has a gift for bargaining, and helped me haggle the sticker price from around $19,000 to just under $16,000.

I got many compliments on the car when I was shopping or at the car wash. When my grandson Jimmy was very young, he said, "Grandma, I want your car when you have to get rid of it."

I no longer drive, and Jimmy, now 28, did end up buying the car from me. He put in a new stereo system and installed new tires, and now he gets the compliments. It makes me happy that someone else loves it as much as I did—and it still runs like a gem!

MARION HANSON · EVERGREEN PARK, IL

Marion was elated to have the car of her dreams at last—just as she'd always imagined it.

Triumph Saves the Day

Dad's hobby car came through in a clutch.

My father, Steven Roper, was an engineer, and he really liked to keep busy. He was always tinkering with something, such as this 1957 Triumph TR3 that he restored.

My father's first Triumph was a powder blue 1954 TR2, but he had some difficulty getting replacement parts for it. To keep it running, he purchased this TR3 for parts. When he bought it, the TR3 was black, and had been retrofitted with a roll bar. Dad removed the roll bar and began restoring the car, which he came to love.

He drove the Triumph mostly to work at first, and then it became his date car. When he began dating my mother, Alma, who at that time lived on a cobblestone road, he picked her up in his Chevy Impala so the street wouldn't damage his baby's suspension. They'd switch to his flashy sports car to cruise.

My parents held on to the Triumph when they bought their first house and started a family. But at some point, Dad made the difficult decision to sell it in order to help provide for his growing family. He repainted it cherry red, knowing it would sell immediately.

This year, at Dad's 80th birthday, we had the image of him, Mom and my oldest sister, Theresa, in the car in 1968 reproduced on a cake. That's when I learned another story about my dad's beloved Triumph.

My brother Stevie was born with a rare genetic disease and was frequently ill. One winter night when Stevie had pneumonia, my parents needed to get him to the hospital quickly, but their main car—the "reliable" one—wouldn't start.

Despite the frigid Pittsburgh weather, the Triumph started. Thanks to it—and my dad's hard work fixing it—my parents were able to drive my brother to the hospital without delay. Not only did they get to the hospital in record time, they also arrived in style! Dad's fun hobby helped save my brother's life.

AMY DANCHISKO · IRWIN, PA

The Triumph has room for Steve, Alma and oldest daughter, Theresa, in 1968.

Everybody In!

On my fifth birthday, in 1951, I was in the driver's seat of the little car my
dad made. The neighborhood kids piled in, too.

DAVID FRIETAS · RENO, NV

CHAPTER 8

SEEING
STARS

Memories of meeting celebrities and
personal heroes lasted a lifetime.

Get Back!

New York police struggle to hold the line against rabid fans of
The Beatles frantic to glimpse the Fab Four outside the Warwick Hotel
in 1965. The band stayed there before an Aug. 15 show at Shea Stadium.

Bob Hope Rounds the Bases

No matter the danger, he gave
them something to smile about.

Hope entertains a military crowd in the South Pacific in 1944.

From his first USO show in 1941 to his last in 1990, Bob Hope forged powerful bonds with troops at home and abroad. They wrote to him as they would write to their own loved ones. In this excerpt from *Dear Bob: Bob Hope's Wartime Correspondence with the G.I.s of World War II*, we see the special place Hope occupied in the hearts of those bearing up in service to their country. Our feature includes firsthand accounts from *Reminisce* readers who saw Bob Hope in Asia in the 1960s. Their memories are still vivid and flooded with the joy of those long-ago moments, and they are fitting tributes to a man who, for 50 years, brought some fun to places where laughter was all too rare.

Sailors serving in the Korean War lift Bob Hope during a show.

On Aug. 12, 1944, while Bob Hope was broadcasting his radio show from a naval hospital in the South Pacific, he quipped: "We have a nice show here with Frances Langford, Jerry Colonna, Tony Romano, Patty Thomas and Barney Dean. I know you'll enjoy the girls. You remember girls?"

The soldiers laughed and cheered. Bob Hope had hit on yet one more familiar aspect of a soldier's misery—the severe, crippling shortage of potential sweethearts. Knowing this, Bob always brought along a handful of pretty gals to entertain the troops and remind them what they were fighting for. Then, he would joke about his unwavering commitment to his work: "It's a tough job, but someone's got to do it."

21ST RECONNAISSANCE TROOP
AMERICAN DIVISION
APO 716 C/O POSTMASTER
SAN FRANCISCO, CALIFORNIA
U.S. ARMY

Dear Bob,

We could call you Mr. Hope, but as we have a favor to ask of you, we want to be good buddies.

If your fan mail is as bad as we have heard, we should be in the same "foxhole," 'cause the women do not write to us either. We thought that you could raise our morale by getting us a few pictures of young and upcoming actresses. We were going to write to Chaplin or Flynn, but we thought they would be having enough on their hands.

I guess you know we think your pictures are great and would like to have more of them out this way

BEST-LAID PLANS

DURING THE VIETNAM WAR, I was stationed at Nakhon Phanom, Thailand (NKP), as the air traffic control tower crew chief. In the fall of 1966, we learned the Bob Hope USO tour was making a stop at our base.

Because military bases have to operate around the clock—and because Bob Hope was such a big deal—command decided to fly a few of us to another base to see an earlier show so we could be on duty while the rest of our base attended the performance.

Despite this plan, a few people missed part of the show that day anyway. During the performance, a plane skidded across the runway on landing and crashed into a ditch. No one was hurt, but I had to call a crash crew, an ambulance and security police; those guys didn't catch the rest of the acts.

That was a shame, because the show was excellent. It did a lot to lift the spirits of everyone who saw it.

CHARLES BURKE · EASLEY, SC

BACKSTAGE WITH A HERO

WHEN BOB HOPE TOURED VIETNAM in December 1969, I was with the 48th Transportation Group based at Long Binh, and among a lucky few chosen to chauffeur for performers during their visit to the 1st Infantry Division base camp at Lai Khe. Even luckier for me, I was assigned to drive for the Gold Diggers—18 beautiful young singers and dancers. It was a thrill, but not quite the highlight of the occasion.

At Lai Khe, while waiting backstage, I noticed a man standing by himself. I strolled over for a chat. As I got closer, I realized it was Neil Armstrong. I excused myself for intruding, but he smiled and motioned me over. He seemed to enjoy answering this common soldier's questions about his famous experience. The ink has blurred a bit on the autograph he gave me, but it still is a treasured keepsake, and the incident remains one of my favorite memories.

STEVE TUNNELL · SOMERVILLE, TX

… *in between your pictures our morale drops—that is why we want you to do this little favor for us to keep our morale at a high level in between your pictures. We would appreciate this very much.*

We sincerely hope that you can accomplish this mission that we are sending you on.

Waiting patiently,
BILL PACHECO, WALLY ENZ AND BEN YANISH

"Here we are, doing the first broadcast from the Hollywood Canteen. Boy, this is really a marvelous place. Can you imagine all those beautiful hostesses and only servicemen are allowed? I know one guy who got dressed up in a uniform so that he could get into the Canteen. But they knew he was a fake because the uniform fit him. So, they threw me out."

BOB HOPE

Left: Jerry Colonna was a regular on Hope's tours in the 1940s. Bottom: Soldiers laugh during a Bob Hope show in Seoul, South Korea, in 1950.

JUNE 27, 1944
BILL PACHECO
21ST RECONNAISSANCE TROOP

Dear Bill, Wally and Ben:

The thought of you boys way out there in some forgotten foxhole without a "pin-up" girl between the three of you haunted my dreams last night. So early this morning I crept up to my attic and, with tears in my eyes, unpinned some of my most prized "pin-ups" to send you fellows. Take good care of them!

I'm glad you like my pictures. I like them, too, which makes four of us. I've just finished two more ... The Road to Utopia for Paramount, and The Princess and the Pirate for Goldwyn. My friends say that the best thing about my pictures is the title.

I expect to leave on a tour of the South Pacific very soon now. May even get a chance to drop in on you boys, so watch out for me. In the meantime, take good care of those "pin-ups," will you?

The "Pin-Up" Collector,

BOB HOPE

"When word got out that we had 10 girls with us, a squadron of fellas flew out to meet us—and some of them even had planes."

BOB HOPE

23 MAY 1944, ENGLAND

Dear Bob,

You were swell enough to send another crew your picture, so now you have another eager beaver after you for another one. Our crew is flying B-24—oh-oh! Was just about to give the number, but happened to think that they would censor that. We are fed up with pin-up girls (Ha! Who said that? That's the funniest thing I've said all day!), and now I'd like to pin you up. We always get a bang out of hearing you, the only trouble is that we don't get to hear you enough.

Lots of good luck to you always,
Another fan—

BILL JONES

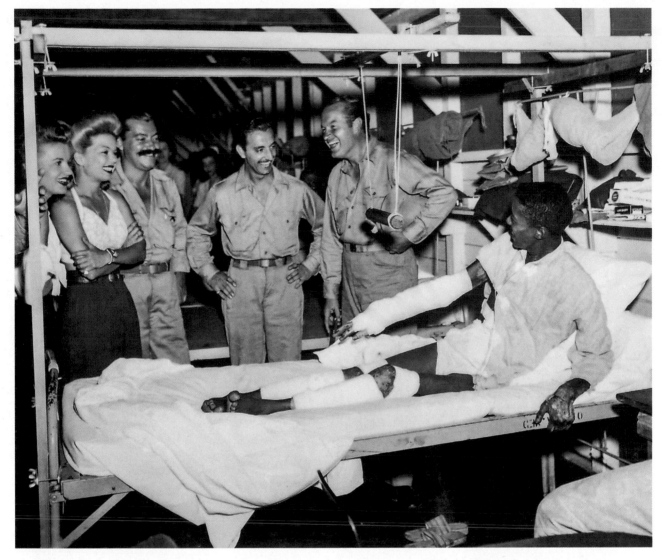

USO stars, including singer Frances Langford, second from left, share a joke with hospital patient Staff Sgt. Johnnie B. Tobbs, in the South Pacific in 1944

"One soldier went to the Hollywood Canteen and danced with Hedy Lamarr, Betty Grable and Lana Turner. I don't know if it affected him or not, but he was a little late getting back to camp. It was Tuesday before an anti-aircraft unit in San Diego could shoot him down."

BOB HOPE

JUNE 22, 1944
SGT. WM. E. JONES,
39559624 838 SQ. 487 BOMB GP.
APO 559, C/O POSTMASTER
NEW YORK, NEW YORK

Dear Bill:

Was very glad to hear from you and, since you asked for it, am forwarding a pin-up of myself. I've had many requests for my picture—the fellas say that when they start feeling low, they go take a look at my picture and realize how lucky they are. I've been quite busy lately. Bing and I have been playing a lot of golf benefits. I've always wondered why they had those flags on the course, but after a couple of shots of mine I found out: That's to tell you what country you're in.

Will have to sign off now and get back to work. Tell the rest of the crew "hello" for me, will you? And the best of good luck to all of you.

Sincerely,

BOB HOPE

"A lot of these Waves wear X-ray equipment. And it is sure convenient for 'em. If a sailor asks 'em for a date, they can look through his pockets and tell if he can afford it or not."

BOB HOPE

Clockwise from top: Raquel Welch invites lucky GIs on stage in Vietnam in 1967. Bob hugs Ann-Margret in 1968. Neil Armstrong greets soldiers in Long Binh, Vietnam, in December 1969.

Years later, I'd mention to friends that I saw Bob Hope on Christmas Day in Vietnam and many were incredulous ("Yeah, sure, everyone says that"). But it was true.

DAVID MEZZERA • VALLEJO, CA

UNITED STATES NAVAL HOSPITAL,
SAN DIEGO, CA

Dear Bob (Have a Heart) Hope:

From the Union 000 of Organized Wolves, we protest to your visiting the Nurses and Waves at the U.S.N.H., as they will not look at us Corpsmen since you have been here.

The poor little dears have been in a flutter and a daze for the last 24 hours.

The next time, please bring along Dot Lamour, Betty Grable, Paulette Goddard, Lana Turner, Gene Tierney and as many more of the gorgeous stars as you can. In that way, making them jealous, we can protect our interest in these organizations.

Maybe it would help to leave Cary Grant at home. It's a flip of a coin to tell which one of you stirred up the commotion. Excuse me, let's flip for odd man, maybe Colonna could take some of the votes.

Anyway, we enjoyed your program and we did get some laughs out of it, even if we can't please the young ladies. So come back again.

Your Fellow Wolves,

THE CORPSMEN
UNITED STATES NAVAL HOSPITAL
SAN DIEGO, CALIFORNIA

Bob Hope's closing tribute to the WACs on his weekly radio show:

"You know, ladies and gentlemen, before we leave tonight I'd like to say how really fine this set-up is here at Fort Des Moines. You know, we may kid a little about the WACs, but believe me, these girls aren't kidding. They're doing a job to be proud of…"

9 MAY 1943
SOMEWHERE IN ENGLAND

Dear Bob:

Received your picture today, after it traveled all over the British Empire. I guess that is why you had such a tired look on your face.

Bob, why don't you give up trying to get Dorothy Lamour and give these English girls a chance? (They like anyone that even resembles a man.) All you have to do is brush up on your English accent and learn to drink tea.

Well, it's 11 o'clock (2300 hours) and I've just finished my day's work at the canteen, so I guess I had better get in my mattress-less, spring-less, sheet-less, sleep-less bed. (Very comfy, though).

A-SOLDIER-IN-THE-REAR-RANK

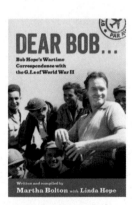

"Dear Bob … We Can Dream, Can't We?" from *Dear Bob … Bob Hope's Wartime Correspondence with the G.I.s of World War II* written and compiled by Martha Bolton with Linda Hope, published by University Press of Mississippi, Copyright © 2021 by the Bob & Dolores Hope Foundation. All rights reserved.

RELIEF IN
A TENSE PLACE

IN EARLY 1964, I flew commercial and military aircraft from North Carolina to South Korea.

In South Korea, the Army assigned me to Camp Casey, situated along the likely invasion route out of North Korea, a few miles from the DMZ.

That December, Bob Hope brought his USO show to Camp Casey.

With him were five of the most beautiful women that I had ever seen, including Miss World and the actress Jill St. John. At the

end of the show, Hope sang his signature tune, "Thanks for the Memory." As he left the stage, I wanted to leap to my feet and shout, "Take me with you!"

I didn't of course, but I longed to be home for Christmas, as did most of my fellow soldiers.

I sometimes think about all the military personnel that Bob Hope entertained in his career—how he brought smiles to thousands of people, if only for fleeting moments. What I do know is only a few memories in a person's life are truly special. That show in 1964 is one such memory for me.

IVAN NICHOLSON · BEMIDJI, MN

ANGST IN AUGUST

In postwar years, summer ends
in melodrama.

1945 »

Conquering Talker

This bit of gee-whiz hit theaters
just as WWII was ending. Fred
MacMurray is flying ace Eddie
Rickenbacker, who entertains
his fellow plane-crash survivors
with tales of his amazing life.
Inspirational? Yes. Tone-deaf?
Also yes.

« 1949

French Twist

With the real drama of
World War II having left
France in shambles, the
romantic entanglements of
a 19th-century housewife seem
oddly innocent. This was the
second time Oklahoma-born
Jennifer Jones played a French
native, after her Oscar-winning
turn as the child who saw holy
visions at Lourdes in *The Song
of Bernadette* (1943).

COLUMBIA PICTURES presents

Anna Lucasta

starring

PAULETTE
GODDARD

William   John   Oscar
Bishop · Ireland · Homolka

AND

BRODERICK
CRAWFORD

Screen Play by Philip Yordan and
Arthur Laurents · Based upon the play,
"Anna Lucasta", by Philip Yordan
A SECURITY PICTURES Production

Directed by IRVING RAPPER · Produced by PHILIP YORDAN

A startling and powerful motion picture version of the stage play which created such great dramatic furore throughout the world

2

1949   **When Bad Girls Happen to Good Guys**

Paulette Goddard stars as a woman set up by her greedy brother-in-law to trick a nice farmer out of his savings. Philip Yordan's play had been around since the mid-1930s, but this version closely follows a successful 1944 American Negro Theater staging that ran for 957 performances.

Spur of the Moment Interview

Bumping into some fans, Dick Clark didn't miss a beat.

———

Seeing celebrities in New York is not uncommon, but the time I saw Dick Clark stands out.

I was working in New York as a financial analyst for the Life Savers Candy Co. One day in 1982, I was waiting in front of 40 W. 57th St. for a group of friends with whom I was going out to lunch.

Down the sidewalk came Dick Clark, with a stunning young woman. She looked like a model and most likely was an aspiring actress as well. Three teenagers came from the opposite direction, noticed Clark, and called his name.

He could have gotten away with a polite nod or a quick hello. Instead, he stopped and talked with them. He asked what kind of music they liked and who their favorite artists were, where they went to school and what sports teams they followed.

The model looked rather annoyed, but Clark and the kids were utterly engrossed in their conversation. There were no press people with Clark, and no one was filming him, so he wasn't putting on a show for anyone. Clark seemed genuinely interested in talking with the kids—and not at all in a condescending manner.

After they finished speaking, he shook hands with each of the teenagers and thanked them for the conversation.

The teenagers continued down the sidewalk talking excitedly with each other; one of them literally jumped up and down.

As Clark and the model walked off, he was smiling from ear to ear, although she didn't look as happy.

GREGORY FARRELL · BASKING RIDGE, NJ

Eternally youthful Dick Clark had an ear for what kids wanted to hear.

Barry Williams, best known as *Brady Bunch* heartthrob Greg, sang and played guitar for the contest winners.

For the Groovy Guy Who Has Everything

Barry Williams brings up a big old bunch of emotions.

The *Brady Bunch* was one of my favorite TV series. In 1973, when I was 12, I entered a radio contest to meet the actor who played Greg Brady, Barry Williams, who was performing at the Steel Pier in Atlantic City, New Jersey.

I was overjoyed when the station called to tell me I was a winner!

I spent the next week excitedly preparing to meet my teen idol. On the big day, I wore a robin's-egg blue halter top with matching flared pants, and did my long hair like many of the other girls of my generation—parted straight down the middle.

I was one of a dozen fans taken to a private area backstage at the Steel Pier. We were brimming with excitement, as were our mothers waiting nearby, many of whom also had sizable crushes on Greg Brady.

Finally, Williams walked into the semicircle we had formed. He was 19, tall and handsome, and dressed in jeans, a T-shirt from *The Exorcist* and a brown suede fringe jacket. He was the epitome of mid-'70s teenage cool, and when we saw him, we all absolutely melted.

He played guitar for us, posed for pictures with us and patiently signed autograph after autograph. Through it all, we were tongue-tied.

I begged and pleaded with my mother to bring me back the next day for Williams' performance at the Golden Dome Ballroom. He gave an excellent concert, and after the show, when he came out to greet his fans, I walked up and gave him a pewter stein that I'd had engraved, "To Barry Williams, with all my love, Theresa Schalk." His fans oohed and aahed as he gave me a big hug, and then a kiss—my first. I was floored!

Decades have passed, but I'll never forget that magical moment.

THERESA TAYLOR • SAN DIEGO, CA

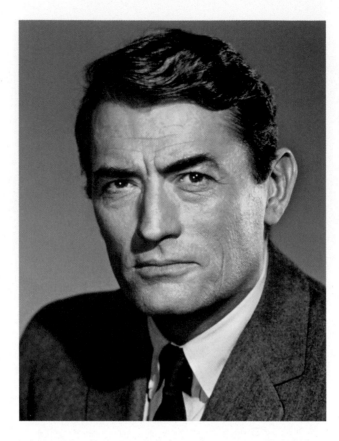

Gregory Peck's best-known movie roles were as the good guy, fighting for decency and justice.

Long-Distance from Hollywood

Gramma approved of Mr. Peck.

—

From before 1950 until her death in 1967, my grandmother Myrtle Gruber lived on a farm east of Elkhart, Indiana. Bordering her property was a heavily traveled section of highway called Toledo Road. It had a sharp curve that was the site of many accidents.

One night in the early 1960s, a car missed the unmarked curve and overturned in the field. Word filtered out that one of Gregory Peck's sons was involved in the crash, and that he and a friend had been taken to Goshen Hospital—farther away than the larger Elkhart General. We assumed the legendary actor's press agent managed a news blackout, and guessed that after being released from the hospital, the men were whisked to the airport in South Bend, or even Chicago.

We visited Gramma soon after the crash, and, she casually said, "A very nice man named Peck called me from California and thanked me for helping his boy last week."

Stunned, one of us blurted, "Do you mean Gregory Peck?" Gramma, who used phrases like "Heavenly days!" and "For land sakes!" and always answered with an upward lilt to her voice, said, "Well, yes?"

And did she know who that was? Gramma probably hadn't been to a motion picture since World War I. She rarely watched TV or read anything but local news. She related that two young men had knocked and asked to use her telephone because they'd had an accident. The boys were "well brought up," reversing the phone charges to their folks. She helped them locate an ambulance service and gave them a snack. A couple of days later the "nice Mr. Peck" called, thanking her—in that deep voice known to millions—for assisting his son and the friend.

To which Gramma replied, "Well, land sakes, I only did what any mother would have done."

STUART GRUBER · MISHAWAKA, IN

Wyatt Earp at Cape Canaveral

Hugh O'Brian marshaled kids to study science.

While I was growing up in South Philadelphia, Pennsylvania, in the 1950s, I looked forward every week to watching *The Life and Legend of Wyatt Earp*. I was a big fan of the show's star, Hugh O'Brian.

More than a decade later, I got to work with him when I was a NASA public affairs contractor at the Kennedy Space Center in Merritt Island, Florida. O'Brian ran a youth leadership organization for students interested in community service and science. The foundation organized weeklong trips to Cape Canaveral so the students could meet astronauts, along with the ground personnel who helped them rocket into space.

I coordinated some of the activities for the groups, including setting up photography sessions with O'Brian and the youthful participants for their hometown news releases. When O'Brian visited my building to plan for the influx of students, he generated a lot of excitement. Workers clamored to catch a glimpse of the Hollywood star. He was friendly and had a good sense of humor.

On one memorable occasion, my wife, Enid, and I spent time with him socially when we attended a NASA reception honoring those of us whose work supported the space program. The honorees also watched an Apollo manned lunar launch from the VIP viewing area.

I was at the Kennedy Space Center for more than eight years; I'm thankful I had the chance to meet and work with O'Brian and his foundation.

STEVE MILNER · YORKTOWN, VA

Steve snapped a shot of a glowing Enid with Hugh O'Brian at a 1972 reception for Apollo program workers.

Life with Loretta

A writer recalls the special time she spent with
golden age screen legend Loretta Young as they
worked on her biography.

JOAN WESTER ANDERSON

Clockwise from top left: Her career took off when she was 14 with *Naughty But Nice* (1927); with her sister Sally Blane in the early 1930s; Loretta at age 4..

W hat was I doing here? I looked beyond the guest room to the backyard pool. I had been invited by Loretta Young, one of my screen idols, to stay with her in her house in Palm Springs, California, for as long as I wanted. A staunch Catholic and voracious reader, she had discovered the books I write about angels and miracles, and felt we were meant to meet. I learned later that as soon as she heard of my work, she was already wondering if I would write her biography.

When she approached me about it, my initial response was a resounding no, followed by "Why me?" Surely screenwriters or freelancers far more able than I could handle a project like this.

Then again, maybe not.

"This book needs to be about my faith as well as my movies and television shows," Loretta said. "This is what you write about, isn't it, dear? Walking the walk? Healing?"

Well, yes. But I wasn't experienced as a biographer. That kind of journalism requires a special skill, and Loretta's long and amazing career deserved the best.

"You'd be taking a chance with me," I told her. "I've never done anything like this."

"Neither have I, dear," came her gentle answer. "Couldn't we learn together?"

My husband, Bill, a longtime fan of Young's, nearly pushed me out the door. "You'd be crazy not to go," he pointed out. "At least see if you like each other. You can always come home." It was a less-than-ringing endorsement, but he was probably right. How often did this kind of opportunity come along?

Gracious and Beautiful

Loretta greeted me with a warm hug on the day I arrived in Palm Springs. She was gracious, unexpectedly witty, and still exquisitely beautiful at the age of 86.

Rather than retire ("From what, dear?"), she was downsizing and rearranging her charming but modest home, making it easier for her to remain

She won three Emmys with her popular NBC series in the 1950s. In '55, Young stands with fellow winner Danny Thomas.

independent. (She kept her Oscar and one of her Emmys on a kitchen shelf next to the coffee tin as reminders of her old life.)

She also was hoping that this biography would put the finishing touches on a life somewhat battered, but well lived.

"Dear Joan," she wrote in a note that she left for me one evening, "You do the work—I'll do the praying. Love, Loretta."

How could I refuse?

Work, Food, Fun
Loretta and I had done some preliminary research before we actually met, so we were vaguely aware of the massive job that awaited us. We soon developed a routine—work, food and fun, in that order, interspersed with naps when necessary.

Loretta was a night owl (I often wondered when she did sleep) and was also timid about using electronic devices, a condition I understand and

share. Given these limits, I showed her how to turn my ancient tape recorder on or off when she got emotional, in case our conversations became too personal. Chatting at our own pace helped clear any trust issues. Some difficult talks were yet to come.

But we knew from the beginning that everything had to be open if she was to achieve her goal of a book that shared both her shadows and joy.

So many years had passed, and witnesses were gone. Memories had dimmed. What to tell. What to delete. How to verify the truth of a particular story. Each day brought its own challenges.

Friends and Fashion
Not everything was work, however. Loretta had an amazing list of friends, of all ages and places, whom she sincerely loved and wanted to keep in her fold. Her local pals were always nearby, ready for a quick trip to the outlet malls if needed.

Her desk was a real fire hazard, piled high with fan correspondence that never seemed to stop. Loretta's housekeeper was unflappable; she routinely shopped and cooked for dinner guests at the drop of a hat. It was like going to a party every night. Loretta and I also learned a kind of verbal shorthand to save time.

Joan: Loretta, do you remember the woman who kept taking pictures of you at the festival?
Loretta: Hmm. Was she wearing a yellow Givenchy?
Joan: Never mind. I'll look it up.

Loretta had such a finely tuned fashion sense that she kept track of how and where her designer clothes were used. Her gowns became a point of reference. I frequently looked up gowns labeled and stored in her garage. After daily Mass she would sometimes visit patients in a nearby hospice unit, holding them in her arms and whispering words of comfort. The two worlds, glamorous star and devoted comforter, collided rarely because she was a remarkable woman—a holy woman—who was able to keep many balls in the air.

And I was feeling inadequate again.

About that Dented Chevy

I decided to talk to Loretta about those feelings after Mass, and joined her as she was pulling out of the garage on her way to the hospital. Her huge 20-year-old Chevrolet Caprice station wagon—boat, more like—was heavily dented. As her friends acknowledged, Loretta was a terrible driver. She rarely cleared her driveway without knocking over a trash can, and she was known for ignoring red lights.

Fortunately, the hospital was close, and we chatted comfortably as we drove along. I noticed a four-way stop ahead; a car facing us had already come to a halt, the driver preparing to make a left turn. Loretta, however, showed no sign of slowing. I gripped the armrest as she sailed right into the intersection and the other driver slammed on his brakes, just missing us. She swerved around him, came to a stop, then looked at me and smiled.

"See? This is why I love Palm Springs," she said. "Everyone here is so friendly. They all wave at me!"

"Loretta," I murmured, "I don't think that man was waving at you."

"Perhaps not," she said, and I caught the twinkle in her beautiful blue eyes. "But, dear, isn't life all in the way you look at it?"

STEEL BUTTERFLY

Joan Anderson describes Loretta Young's life as "battered, but well lived." It was often chaotic, with exultant highs and despondent lows.

She was born Gretchen Micheala in Salt Lake City in 1913, one of four children—three girls and a boy—of Gladys and Earl Young. Her parents separated when she was 3; Gladys moved the kids to Hollywood, California, where she opened a boarding house.

Young started in bit parts in films before she turned 5. Her big break came at age 14, when she landed a supporting role in *Naughty But Nice* (1927).

Her delicate beauty and easygoing persona on screen belied Young's toughness and ambition. Her first husband, Grant Withers, called her "a steel butterfly." She balked at the control studios exerted on stars. She refused a contract for $2 million from studio executive Darryl Zanuck—which angered him so much that he had her blackballed for a time.

After 20 years as an actor, Young finally won an Academy Award for portraying a Swedish maid who runs for Congress in *The Farmer's Daughter* (1947).

Always a devout Catholic, Young had a reputation for moralizing. She set up a curse jar on set and sent the proceeds to a home for unwed mothers. Her good friend Barbara Stanwyck called her Attila the Nun.

Young had a baby by Clark Gable in 1935. After putting the child in an orphanage for a year, Young adopted the girl, Judy, who didn't learn the truth of her birth until she was in her 30s—though the story was rampant rumor in Tinseltown for years. Young always denied it until at last confirming the story to Anderson in *Forever Young*, which published after Young died.

MARY-LIZ SHAW

A devout Catholic, Young supported many church charities. In 1954, she went to the groundbreaking of a new maternity hospital.

Loretta had an amazing list of friends,
of all ages and places.

In the way you look at it. I had never thought of it like that.

Loretta's view of her life was her choice, and filling her heart and soul with goodness and grace enabled her to live that life, despite setbacks. It was something to think about.

Loretta Forever

I came home to write, research and interview, and I had been mailing Loretta chapters as they took shape. One day in late May 2000, Loretta asked quite unexpectedly if I would come back to Palm Springs.

"I'm not feeling very well right now, and you and I have a few more details to discuss."

We were so close to the end of our book, *Forever Young.* We even found a publisher (Thomas More) willing to extend our deadline.

But our reunion never took place. She worsened and went into the hospital for the last time. I finished the few remaining details and canceled the media interviews I had hoped she could handle. I should be despondent, I realized, but instead I felt buoyant, even joyful. I knew where Loretta was and that I would see her again.

"Couldn't we learn together?" she once asked me. I think we did.

Forever Young: The Life, Loves and Enduring Faith of a Hollywood Legend by Joan Wester Anderson was published in 2000.

Clothes were another passion; her third husband was costume designer Jean Louis.

Clooney's career spanned music, TV and film, culminating in a Grammy Lifetime Achievement Award in 2002.

Christmas in July

Rosemary Clooney offered poolside refreshment.

Two nights a week and on Saturday mornings I tended the switchboard at the Art Center School in Los Angeles (now the ArtCenter College of Design). It was the early 1960s, and I was studying photography. The switchboard job was easy duty, and I could use the extra money.

One evening in July, Fred Lyon, a photographer in San Francisco and an Art Center alum, called the switchboard. He was looking for an assistant for a photo shoot, and wondered if the school could help.

In fact, I did think the school could find him an assistant—me!

I met him in the lobby of the Beverly Hills Hotel the next Sunday morning. His assignment was to shoot Rosemary Clooney and Jose Ferrer and their five children for the Christmas spread in a magazine.

We went to their house in Beverly Hills, and Lyon posed the family on the stairway, which was decorated with Christmas bows and holly.

Clooney was a gracious host, and asked us if we would like to sit by the pool and have an iced tea. She couldn't have been more accommodating or charming; Ferrer, not so much. He made only a quick appearance and then left.

The Art Center was wonderful, and it prepared me well for my career. I graduated in January 1961 and moved with my wife and daughter to Detroit, Michigan. I worked at a studio for a few years before opening my own place, eventually retiring with the advent of digital photography.

Interestingly, on the same day that I assisted Lyon with the Clooney assignment, we also went to the home of Robert Stack for another shoot.

Stack was in the TV series *The Untouchables*, which was very popular. Like Clooney, he was gracious, and he was eager to show us his new Hasselblad, a beautiful and expensive Swedish camera. I saw Stack again years later in Los Angeles. For good reason, he didn't remember me.

BENNETT YOUNT · ORCHARD PARK, NY

HOLLYWOOD STARS

ROOTING FOR THE RAT PACK

Peter Lawford, Dean Martin, Sammy Davis Jr. and Frank Sinatra were rogues worth cheering for in *Ocean's 11*.

WEDDED BLISS

Lauren Bacall, Betty Grable and Marilyn Monroe are models with money in mind in the 1953 hit *How to Marry a Millionaire*. Rory Calhoun was a target, despite his slim wallet.

THEY PACKED UP THE TRUCK

Rich on "Texas tea," TV's Clampetts cruise Los Angeles in *The Beverly Hillbillies*, which started its nine-season run on CBS in 1962.

Jackie Robinson On First

At Ebbets Field with Dad, she saw a hero in the making.

O n game days during baseball season, my father, Benjamin Levin, and I sat in the living room listening to our home team, the Brooklyn Dodgers, on the radio. Sometimes we took the long bus ride to Ebbets Field, arriving early to watch batting practice from the outfield.

In 1947, when I was 13, we'd been hearing for weeks about a talented young Black player the Dodgers had signed. The team finally announced that Jackie Robinson would play his first major league game on Tuesday, April 15.

My father and I were at Ebbets Field that day, along with more than 26,000 other fans. The crowd seemed tentative as Robinson took the field, but I sensed something special was happening. Though he went on to be the Dodgers' second baseman, Robinson played first base that day. He didn't get a hit, but he got on base on an error in the seventh inning, and scored the run that gave Brooklyn the lead on the way to a win.

I admired the inner strength Robinson showed during his career as he played his way through taunts and threats, and then went on to become active in the civil rights movement. My beloved Dodgers went to California in 1958, and when my husband and I later moved to Florida, I adopted the Marlins as my team. I even threw out the first pitch at one of their games.

One can't always recognize momentous occasions as they occur, but something special did happen that Tuesday in 1947. Being there and getting to share that piece of history with my dad is something I'll never forget.

MINDY BROTHERS · ATLANTA, GA

Mindy was a fan of the Brooklyn Dodgers when Jackie Robinson began playing for the team in 1947. Years later, after moving to Florida, she cheered for the Marlins.

Jesse Owens joined Jackie's parents, Evelyn and Chester, at an Oregon track event in the 1930s.

Running with the Best

Her father befriended track legend Jesse Owens.

My father, Chester E. Page, did a lot of track and field in his teens and early 20s and won several trophies. during that time, he met and became friends with Jesse Owens.

In the early 1930s, when I was just a toddler, my father invited Owens to a sporting event in Salem, Oregon, where we were living. I treasure a picture taken around that time of Owens with my dad and mother, Evelyn.

My father liked to show off his prowess by jumping over our car while it was parked at the beach. I inherited some of his track talent; I was a fast runner as a teenager. Uncle Raymond, Dad's brother, decided that I should compete in the pre-Olympic trials, despite my being a smoker and having no training. Dad wanted nothing to do with this endeavor.

I managed to come in second in the heats, which were run on a straightaway, and qualified for the 200-meter finals. When he heard that, Dad showed up to see my race.

I was in the outside lane and took off feeling pretty confident, but as we headed into the curve, I suddenly found myself in last place. I was so deeply embarrassed that I ran completely off the track and hid behind the popcorn stand while the other runners passed the bleachers where my father was sitting. I never lived that down.

At least Dad didn't invite Owens to that event! Sadly, I have no memory of meeting Owens when I was a child, but my parents always remembered him as friendly and down-to-earth.

JACQUELYNE PAGE-DAMATO
SAN FRANCISCO, CA

A baseball signed by Babe Ruth was Ray Sr.'s souvenir of a once-in-a-lifetime meeting. Some signed Babe Ruth baseballs can sell for more than $100,000 today.

Special Gift from the Babe

Baseball fan treasured meeting an icon of the game.

M y dad, Ray Cauwet Sr., who died several years ago at age 93, had a cherished recollection of meeting Babe Ruth in 1923.

Dad grew up in the Mission District of San Francisco, and was an avid baseball fan all his life.

He and his father went to every game played by the San Francisco Seals in the Pacific Coast League. Two of the team's stars, Paul and Lloyd Waner, lived next door. The Waner brothers played for the Seals in the early 1920s before moving to the major leagues. Both outfielders, they were amazing hitters. Paul and Lloyd were later elected to the Baseball Hall of Fame.

In addition to his love of the Seals, my dad was a devoted fan of the New York Yankees, particularly the player who wore No. 3, Babe Ruth. Dad read every account of Ruth's exploits that he could find.

It turned out that Paul Waner and Ruth were friends. In 1923, when the Babe stopped by the Waners' for a visit, Paul invited my dad over. Dad was almost speechless, but he managed to tell Babe how much he admired him and asked him to sign a ball. Dad went home with his prize and a memory that would last a lifetime. Years later, he got to see the Babe in action during the 1932 World Series, when the Yankees played the Chicago Cubs. Dad was among the lucky fans at the now-famous Game 3, when in the fifth inning Babe appeared to point at center field on a 2-2 count. On the next pitch, he slammed a home run to center field.

Dad's signed ball held a flood of memories for him, especially of a day when a baseball great chose to spend time with an 11-year-old kid.

RAY CAUWET II · PORTERVILLE, CA

Lucky Find on the Campaign Trail

Hubert Humphrey's loss (of a tie clip)
was a win for one constituent.

During the hotly contested 1968 presidential election, Vice President Hubert Humphrey, the Democratic presidential nominee, made two trips to the Lehigh Valley in Pennsylvania. The valley is a large population center that includes Allentown, Bethlehem, Easton and surrounding communities, and with unionized companies like Bethlehem Steel and Mack Trucks, it was vital to Humphrey's campaign.

In the usual bustle at the airport, there were a lot of people around Humphrey as he made his way to a waiting car. He gave his speech and returned to the airport to go on to the next stop.

The next morning my father, Edwin, who worked at an Allentown engineering firm, went to the airport to pick up some business associates when something shiny lying by the curb caught his eye. Amazingly, it was Humphrey's tie clasp, which he lost in the jostling the day before.

My father was definitely a Richard Nixon supporter and although I was only 8, I remember staying up late with my parents the night of that election, watching the results trickle in. We all fell asleep after midnight and woke to find Nixon had won. I was probably one of the few fourth graders watching those returns. But it was a sign of things to come because I still love politics.

And more than 50 years later, I still have Humphrey's tie clip.

KEVIN BRADLEY · NORTHAMPTON, PA

Kevin showed an early interest in politics, thanks to his parents, Anna and Edwin.

Twist Again

Ernest Evans, aka Chubby Checker, performs his signature move.
His cover version of Hank Ballard's "The Twist" hit No. 1 in
1960 and again in 1962.